VICTIM TO SURVIVOR

Victim to Survivor

Women

Recovering

from

Clergy

Sexual Abuse

EDITED BY

NANCY WERKING POLING

WIPF & STOCK · Eugene, Oregon

Wipf and Stock Publishers
199 W 8th Ave, Suite 3
Eugene, OR 97401

Victim to Survivor
Women Recovering from Clergy Sexual Abuse
By Poling, Nancy Werking
Copyright©1999 Pilgrim Press
ISBN 13: 978-1-60899-343-7
Publication date 12/14/2009
Previously published by United Church Press, 1999

We, the contributors to this collection,
dedicate the volume to people who have stood by us, especially
Kathy, Daryl, Carolyn, Kris, Mary, Jane, and Howard.

Contents

Foreword

Marie M. Fortune

The stories in this volume are the stories of women who have been sexually abused and exploited by Christian ministers, the very people whom they thought they could trust. Sadly, these stories can be multiplied by the thousands in North America and around the world. To the uninformed reader, they will sound peculiarly similar, perhaps even suspect. They *are* peculiarly similar, but this fact in no way compromises their credibility. Rather, it is merely an indicator of how incredibly consistent are the behaviors of the perpetrators. The consistency of the women's responses to the perpetrators indicates only how each woman struggled to preserve her self and at times her sanity in the midst of the misconduct of her minister and the lack of support from her church.

The miracle of these stories (and the hundreds more like them) is that these women are the church, the broken body of Christ seeking to be made whole through the courage to demand justice. In their pain, these women call upon the church to *be* the church, and they really expect those of us in the institutional church to rise to the occasion. Tragically, all too often we have failed them. We have sent them away with a stone instead of the bread they deserved. Yet often, like the persistent widow in Luke's Gospel (18:2–7), they have gone back again and again to the unjust judge, demanding to be vindicated.

Only occasionally (and I write this with a profound heaviness in my own heart) have such women found a just and compassionate response from their church. All too often they have been blamed, rejected, stigmatized, persecuted, and revictimized. Many have left the church in order to survive. But we must remember that they did not leave voluntarily; they were driven away by an institution that failed in its responsibility to protect its people from the unethical and exploitative practices of its leaders. Those who have left represent a huge loss for us all. Their skills, energy, and faith are no longer available to us for the ministry of the church. A few have stayed, buoyed by a just and reasonable response. Many of these who have stayed now work from the inside to change the practices that they know are so harmful to congregants.

In this volume you will read about women who see themselves as *victims*. To be a victim is to be made temporarily powerless by the actions of another or by a natural disaster. Each of these women at some point was a victim, although there was nothing natural about these disasters. The women were deprived of their usual resources for discernment, good judgment, and action by the behavior of a trusted helper.

Some of the authors refer to themselves as *survivors*. This means that they have begun their journey toward healing and wholeness; they are regaining their sense of self and the ability to act on their own behalf. In short, they have survived against great odds.

Still other authors refer to themselves as *thrivers*. This means that they see themselves as moving beyond having survived the victimization, truly regaining themselves, and getting on with their lives. While they will never forget what happened, it no longer serves as a defining, limiting experience. They take away lessons learned and turn their energies to other parts of their lives.

There are certainly many voices missing here, for example, voices from Christian women in the Philippines and Korea whose stories I have heard, and voices from other religious traditions. We are missing the voices of women who want to tell their stories but cannot at this time for various reasons. We are missing the voices of those women who died by suicide or from illnesses certainly exacerbated by the pain of their victimization. Nonetheless, the voices present here speak eloquently on behalf of themselves and many others.

All of the stories you will read here involve male pastors abusing female congregants. This is certainly the most common scenario that I hear about. But there are some female ministers who abuse both women and men, some male ministers who abuse both women and men, and some ministers who also abuse children and teens. Whatever the specifics, whether Roman Catholic or Protestant, it is wrong for a trusted helper like a minister to be sexually and emotionally intimate with a congregant who is in need of assistance or instruction.

Listen as each woman describes the grooming behavior carried out by her pastor as he broke down her defenses, minimized her questions and concerns, and eventually crossed her sexual boundaries. He made her feel special; he took her seriously, she thought; he mentored her in her vocation for ministry; he isolated her from other people.

Listen for the perpetrators' patterns of behavior. They are disturbingly similar. The perpetrators virtually always have abused other victims. Some of the writers in this book knew there were other women who had been victimized. The others probably just weren't aware of the victims who had preceded them. And there is always the pastor's expectation of secrecy. Keeping the secret protects the offending pastor and isolates the congregant, which makes it difficult for her to sort out what is going on and to ask for help.

Listen for the vulnerability each woman brought to her pastor. The women entrusted their pastors with information about their histories and current situations that should have led the pastors to be especially careful not to take advantage of them. They confided their fears and memories, secrets and confessions, hopes and dreams. They usually came to the pastors in a time of need, such as a health or family crisis, vocational crisis, or spiritual dilemma. These are moments of vulnerability that we all experience at some time or other in our lives. We deserve to be able to entrust these vulnerabilities to a competent, ethical helper. Instead, for these women, their vulnerabilities became the means of exploitation by their pastors.

Listen for the ways that the women struggled with self-blame and a sense of responsibility for what happened. This is usually very difficult for victims. None of us wants to believe that we don't have the power to choose for ourselves. And some of the women clearly made choices early on that they later regretted. What we must remember is that a person's moral agency, that is, her sense of what is right for her and her ability to act on it, is severely compromised when someone she trusts is manipulating her. When the person she regards as her moral guide convinces her that "God has blessed our love," that "this relationship is different and special," that "others would not understand," or that her providing for the sexual needs of the minister is her "contribution to the work of the church," her sense of appropriate behavior with that person goes out the window. Add to that some women's religious training that whatever an ordained person does must be right and good because God does not let a pastor or priest do anything wrong, and it should come as no surprise how easily a pastor can manipulate a congregant into a situation in which the pastor can then cross emotional and sexual boundaries.

Listen to the price these women have paid. Much was stolen from them by the sometimes careless, sometimes malevolent behavior of a pastor. Some no longer are married or partnered; some have not been able to follow the educational or vocational paths they sought; some struggle with alcohol, drugs, or food addictions; most are estranged from their churches. These things were not lost, they were stolen.

Perhaps the most powerful message we can receive from these women is that of their profound faithfulness, courage, and resilience. I am convinced that their love of the church is far greater than mine and their faith in God far deeper than mine. Many of them have stood up to the powers and principalities of the church, have asked for what is rightfully theirs, and have refused to be silent or to disappear. They are, for me, quintessential witnesses to the gospel.

If you have been sexually intimate with your minister or pastoral counselor, supervisor, or seminary professor, I hope you will find some comfort in these pages. Here you will find that you are not alone and that you are not crazy. This can happen to anyone. All it takes is a person who is at a vulnerable point in her life, a pastor who is careless and/or unethical, and a context of secrecy. Unfortunately, when these factors are in place, it is then predictable that the congregant will be taken advantage of.

When these women brought complaints, they met with varying degrees of success. A wide range of responses are possible, from the tragic and outrageous to the good and solid. In my experience, the church is more likely to disappoint than to satisfy the needs of the survivor. But don't let this necessarily discourage you from trying. If and when you are ready, are feeling strong enough to sustain an effort, and have some system of support around you, you may choose to bring a complaint as part of your own healing process. Lower your expectations below what you deserve, and you may be surprised by getting more than you expected.

Go about your healing at your own pace. Listen to the lessons in each woman's experience. The most important thing is to talk with someone whom you feel you can trust. I realize that this is what got you into this situation in the first place, but keep looking. None of us is unconditionally trustworthy, because we all make mistakes. But some therapists, ministers, and friends can be trusted. Tell your story. Let the listener help you see what happened. Educate yourself about the dynamics of pastoral abuse. Try to find other survivors through support groups, retreats, and networks.

If you have been fortunate not to have been exploited by your pastor, then the information you glean from this volume may help open your eyes to the warning signs of an unethical religious leader. If you feel that your pastor is being inappropriate with you, discuss your feelings with a friend or therapist; get a reality check. Then, if your feelings seem true to you, run in the opposite direction. You may also decide to confront the pastor (with a support person) or to report the pastor to the local church or to state or national church authorities. Again, make sure you have the support you will need. I hope the witness of these women will also make you more aware and sympathetic when you hear someone trying to tell her story or if someone brings a complaint against your pastor. Try to put yourself in her place and to understand her experience.

If you are someone who cares about a woman who has been victimized by her minister, I hope you will find a new awareness in these stories that will help you support her in her efforts to find healing. If you are her partner, you may initially feel angry with her and betrayed by her. Educate yourself about the dynamics of pastoral abuse. Remember that her moral agency and choices were compromised by a person she trusted. Remember that although you are in pain, you are not the victim; she is. Find someone to talk with about your pain, but don't take it out on her.

If you are a friend or family member of a woman who has been victimized, let her do her healing at her own pace. Don't offer platitudes and advice; don't tell her she should just forgive and forget and get on with her life. It isn't that easy. You may feel overwhelmed at points by the intensity of her feelings, especially her anger. There will be times when you just don't want to be around her. It's okay for you to take a break, too. Try to understand the pain she is going through. Find ways to hang in there with her as she makes her way along her healing path. Support her initiatives. Be a sounding board. Stand by her side as she seeks justice and healing.

If you are someone who works in the church and carries some degree of responsibility for the adjudication of complaints against ministers who exploit their congregants, I hope these testimonies will help you understand the experience of women who have been abused by a minister and that you will be moved to advocate for them and to call their perpetrators to account. The most important thing you can do is to educate yourself about pastoral misconduct and abuse. Books, videos, and training opportunities abound. If you have a clear understanding of what is going on, grounded scripturally and theologically, you will be much more effective in the actions you undertake.

You will be asked to do three difficult tasks. First, you must determine what happened in a given situation and whether the stated policy of standards for ministers in your judicatory was violated. This is adjudication. Second, you will be asked to stand with the victim/complainant as she seeks justice and healing. Third, you will be asked to call the abusing pastor to account. In so doing, you maximize his or her potential for redemption and you protect others who might be harmed if he or she were allowed to continue representing your church.

You will make mistakes. But if you can maintain a clear vision of your responsibility to call false shepherds to account (see Ezekiel 34) and to protect the vulnerable (see the hospitality code throughout the Hebrew Scriptures and New Testament), you will fulfill your responsibility to protect the church and its people from harm.

For those of us who remain in the church and are committed to making it as safe a place as possible for those who turn to it, we must recognize that the stories we read here (along with many others) are a gift to us. They are the gift of the truth about who we are as church and what we need to do to be faithful to our call to comfort the afflicted and to afflict the comfortable. These women speak truth to power in the hope that they will be heard and that things will be changed. It is a painful truth. As a colleague of mine says (in paraphrasing John 8:32), "You will know the truth, and the truth will make you flinch before it sets you free."

This truth truly makes the powerful in the church flinch. But it can set us all free if we will only listen, take the gospel to heart, and act.

Preface

The six authors had plenty of reasons *not* to write their stories for this volume. Most already had hectic schedules and didn't need yet another deadline. Some lacked confidence in their ability to put their experiences on paper. Nearly all dreaded calling back the memories of one of the most painful and defining periods of their lives. Nevertheless, each woman was eager to take on the project. Over and over I was told, "I want other victims to know they are not alone and that healing comes."

This book is first and foremost for women whose trust has been betrayed by professionals in the helping fields, particularly by clergymen. I am sure the experiences of the authors will inspire and encourage you. For family and friends of women who have been abused, I hope the narratives will lead you to a better understanding of the suffering that clergy sexual abuse brings to its victims. Finally, I encourage church leaders to read this collection so that you can better recognize abusive patterns and can more effectively respond to victims' cries for healing and justice.

As soon as United Church Press approved this project, I knew two women to contact. Needing to fill the other four slots, I began to explore the clergy-abuse network, calling denominational advocates and the Center for the Prevention of Sexual and Domestic Violence. I asked to be put in contact with women abused as adults by clergy—women who had found healing, who understood the dynamics of what had happened to them, and who were articulate in their interpretations. "I could direct you to about a hundred of those," one denominational advocate told me. Perhaps the saddest aspect of this volume is that these six authors represent so many others.

The advocates then contacted women who met the criteria, and the women contacted me. Some who called decided this was not the right time to tell their stories. Two were in the middle of lawsuits and were advised by their attorneys not to write yet about their experiences. For others, the trauma seemed too recent. Someday, they said. The women who agreed to write represent six Christian traditions that span the scale from sectarian to mainline, conservative to liberal. They live in six different states, ranging from the East Coast to the West.

Although I originally established diversity as a goal, that intent was only partially met. Representing ethnic diversity proved a difficult task, perhaps because many cultures do not speak openly about sexual matters and perhaps because of the challenge of quickly building a trusting relationship over the phone. The authors are also not representative in two other respects: four hold advanced degrees, and all have had, at some point, financial resources or insurance to pay for professional therapy.

I asked the authors to consider seven questions:

1. What made you vulnerable?
2. How did the abuser exploit your vulnerability?
3. What was there about your relationship with the abuser that made it a terrible or destructive experience?
4. When and how did you begin to see what was happening to you?
5. How did the church respond? How did these responses affect you?
6. How have you experienced healing?
7. How has this experience affected your relationship with God and/or the church?

Not surprisingly to those who know the field of clergy sexual abuse, the responses to these questions were often similar. So while readers may expect six differing accounts, they will find abusers who share many characteristics, and survivors whose grit and interpretation bear similarities.

The authors have changed all names and have omitted specific references to the churches involved. In one case, where the writer wished to make reference to specific teachings, she named the church's historic tradition. Authors chose their own pen names.

A volume such as this raises many questions: How many victims of clergy sexual abuse are there? What is the full range of experiences? How do we find the voices of those who have died or have left the church? What are the effects on spouses and children of abusers? What are the effects on the families of victims? What are examples of church leaders doing the right thing?

Working with these six women has been an inspiring experience. Over the phone and through E-mail, we have added, deleted, clarified, and sequenced. And we have cried. Every change, every clarification required going back yet again into the painful past. I thank God for each of these women and for each one's courage not only to confront her own abuse but also to become a healing agent for others.

I have been fortunate to meet or to talk by phone with several church leaders, primarily women, who are dedicated to issues of justice and accountability, especially as they relate to clergy sexual abuse. I thank these advocates for their perseverance as well as for the words of support they offered as I began the project. Special thanks also go to the Center for the Prevention of Sexual and Domestic Violence, Marie Fortune, Carolyn Holderread Heggen, Stephanie Anna Hixon, Mildred Myren, and James Poling.

CHAPTER ONE

A Bent-Over Woman Stands Up

Melinda

My understanding of justice has drastically changed. Justice would be for the abuse never to have occurred. But once abuse has taken place, it cannot be undone. No restitution can take back the evil inflicted. My life can never go back to what it was before I experienced the pain of twenty-five years of betrayal and abandonment. I wanted the church, the seminary, the bishop, and others to make it right, yet I had no clue that I was asking the impossible. No one could take back what I had experienced and turn it into a just situation.

My friend's question caught me off guard. I hadn't thought much lately about "if I had it to do over again." That whole episode in my life seemed so long ago, so recent, ancient history, still raw. Would I register a formal complaint of sexual harassment against a highly respected, charismatic (not to mention good-looking) seminary professor and ordained minister? Sitting around the dining room table, enjoying a delicious home-cooked meal, recalling events of the past as well as catching up on happenings of the present, I was unnerved by the question. My answer was halting at best: "Yes . . . maybe . . . I really don't know."

The question stayed with me long after that clear May evening. The pain was still acute, in spite of all the counseling, treatment centers, prayers, and tears. In retrospect, I now realize that I was confronting something much bigger than the experience of one short-lived, indiscreet, abusive relationship. The act of choosing to take back my power from one man to whom it had been surrendered opened a veritable Pandora's box, revealing a lifetime of abuse at the hands of another minister: my husband. While I was seeking justice in one abusive relationship, the lies and betrayals of the other were exposed.

How did this situation come about? How was I to make sense of the seemingly senseless? The answers were not easy to come by. The search opened old wounds, but with that search for meaning, healing was finally allowed to begin.

Todd and I married at an early age. I was nineteen, he twenty-one. I can't say we were hopelessly in love. He thought I would make a good preacher's wife, an asset for a man planning to become a bishop someday. Although young, I was afraid no one else would have me, that this chance might never come around again. Besides, he was exciting. I was dazzled by this charming, charismatic, musically gifted, articulate, good-looking man. His attention swept me—a shy, insecure wallflower—off my feet. Never mind the subtle and not-so-subtle insults. Never mind his overt flirtations with other women. Never mind my own doubts and fears about our relationship. I was convinced that a "good-enough" woman could keep her man. On our wedding day something deep inside alerted me to the fact that I was making a terrible mistake, but I took our marriage vows seriously, believing once married, always married.

There was no honeymoon. Todd wanted to remain in close contact with his friends, so we stayed in a local motel room our first night and returned to our apartment the next day. The second night of our marriage, as I lay in bed beside him, he spoke by phone to an old girlfriend, telling her of his regrets about getting married. Through my tears, I became determined to do whatever it took to *love* him into loving me. Thus began years of proving my steadfastness and loyalty to a man who, despite his vows, never truly wanted to be my husband. Soon after our wedding he enrolled in a conservative evangelical seminary in the South and took a student appointment eighty miles away. There, in his first appointment, the infidelities began.

Todd's first full-fledged affair was with a church school teacher while I was pregnant with our first child. I don't know how I survived the grief of that betrayal, but I did. I prayed for relief from the pain, for the ability to "forgive and forget," for the strength to love him more fully. Maybe then he would not feel the need to turn to other women for solace and support. I believed it was my responsibility to make the marriage last, to make it work at all costs.

I assumed the responsibility for his infidelities. If I were prettier, sexier, more spiritual (I told myself), a better wife, a better mother, a better Christian, he wouldn't have to look elsewhere. So I resolved to be all those things. I became the model wife. I experimented with every beauty secret I could find. I became a vamp in the bedroom and the picture of virtue in public. I spent hours in Bible study and prayer. I fasted for the healing of our marriage. You name it, I did it. In short order we had three children, yet Todd's acting out worsened.

I sought counsel and advice from the clergyman who had officiated at our wedding. He reminded me of the importance of my role as wife and mother, a role God intended to be subservient to the head of the household. He also said it was in the children's best interest for me to remain in a bad—even abusive—marriage. He gently assured me that Todd would begin to settle down as I fell more in line with biblical teachings.

We moved frequently throughout our marriage. We would start off in each new place with high hopes. But it wasn't long before Todd identified the women who might be receptive to his charm, his good looks, his disarming ways, his feigned sincerity. Soon he would again be enmeshed in the lives of the women he pastored, and I would be trying my best to be good enough, big enough, Christian enough to overlook his shortcomings, to forgive the hurts.

I contemplated leaving him many times but found little support from either church or family. Whenever he sensed I might leave, he was quick to remind me that I had no marketable skills with which to make a living. No judge would give me custody of one child, much less three, when the father was a respected minister with a steady income and a manse. I could not, I would not leave the children. Each time Todd and I had this conversation, I renewed my determination to make the marriage work.

The worst years were his years in campus ministry, first in a small regional college in the South, later at a major university in the North. By then I knew I could not compete with the young, nubile women with whom he surrounded himself. He blatantly dated, leaving me home with the kids, then acted the jilted lover when one of his protégées became romantically involved in a more appropriate relationship.

During those years I came to know that sooner or later he would leave me. Rather than wait for that to happen and be left without resources, I returned to school to complete my undergraduate degree. Now in my thirties, I renewed my resolve to make myself marketable. I sensed that to remain dependent on another was a very precarious position, especially for a woman in my situation.

I also began to question the church's teachings about marriage and about women's role in marriage. The "how come" questions, I called them. How come this relationship is my sole responsibility? How come I have to submit to someone who so thoroughly despises me? How come Todd's infidelities are attributed to me? How come . . . How come . . . How come? Somewhere deep inside I knew there was more to life than being a doormat for an abusive man, even if he was a man of the cloth. The rage that had been building within me for years began to be directed toward the church and toward a God who would create a world where such inequity and abuse were sanctioned, even held up as holy and sacred. I could no longer worship such a God. Guilt began to eat at me.

In the early stages of this awareness, I began to discover that I was an intelligent person, a woman of worth and value. Through their teachings, church leaders told me I was vain to like myself, selfish to care about my well-being, heretical to question God or the church. Looking back, I now understand that those messages from the church and from Todd were lies. Slowly over the ensuing years, I began to grasp the notion that I, too, carried the image of God within me. I, too, had a calling, a place of value and worth in this society. I, too, had a voice and took up space—worthy space at that. I, too, was a fully embodied human being, and that in itself was good.

I began to let go of Todd. My early efforts to disentangle from him were clumsy at best, and not altogether healthy. I began to pursue my own life and to ignore what he was doing or what woman he was seeing. At first glance this could be interpreted as a positive step toward reclaiming my sense of worth. It was, to a degree.

However, because staying present in my marriage was so excruciating, I used denial to run away. I did not have the internal tools necessary to recognize and deal with the monumental destructive issues at the heart of our marriage: issues of power and control, of addictions and denial, of dependency and self-loathing. Nor was I able completely to discard deeply ingrained church teachings born of a theology based on a hierarchical understanding of the whole created order. This theology, above all else, prohibited me from leaving the destructive relationship.

I completed my degree. I lost myself in my studies and my children. I became an overprotective mother, fearing that the children, too, would be abused by society in general and the church in particular. Desperately wanting to protect them from the pains I had suffered in life, I became hypervigilant in my parenting. As sad as it is to say, I seldom enjoyed the events of their formative years. I tried to protect them from life as desperately as I had been trying to save Todd's and my marriage.

Gradually I started to "zone out." When Todd called me names, I went numb. When he belittled me in the presence of the children, I disassociated and went to a fantasy place. When he insulted or corrected me in public, I pretended he was talking about someone else, and smiled—I always smiled. When parishioners treated me with disrespect, patronized me, or simply ignored me, I acted like they didn't matter. My involvement in the church lessened over time, and I began to look elsewhere for validation and support. Meanwhile, the pain, in spite of my vehement denial, deepened.

In time I was able to secure a position as director of a women's center. It was during those years that I began to flourish. I became militant in my feminist beliefs. I discovered that I was an articulate and exceedingly strong advocate for abused women, as well as a defender of women's rights. But while I could fight for others, I was still incapable of advocating for myself, of believing I could be or do anything on my own. And more than ever, considering the position I held in the community, I fiercely guarded the family secret. As Todd's behavior continued, my denial isolated me from those who might have provided support and nurture.

Over the years, Todd regularly confessed his sins, offered tearful apologies, promised undying love and, yes, recommitted himself to faithfulness. Each time I forgave, quelled my tears and pain, covered for him, lied for him, and believed him, always hoping that this time things would be different. I hoped and prayed that his repeated repentance would take; that, with God's help, he would emerge as the man I knew he could be. I sought to understand why he was the way he was and believed, as I had been taught, that by my saintly behavior and unabated love he would be healed of that which had so deeply wounded him, that which compelled him to sexualize his relationships with women. Maybe for the sake of our children he would change. Instead of changing, though, he criticized me both for wanting to change him and for wanting to leave him. I was damned if I stayed, damned if I left.

Even deeper than the emotion I interpreted as love for Todd was the sense of myself as a failure if I could not hold the marriage together. I panicked at the thought of being alone, of being a loser, of being perceived as unlovable and incapable in the eyes of the church—and in the eyes of humanity! The notion that I was solely responsible for the marriage still ruled my thoughts and actions.

I continued to hope against all odds that we would have a loving, respectful relationship if only I could figure out the right formula. The harder I tried, however, the worse Todd's behavior became: pornography, prostitutes, phone sex, anonymous men in darkened adult bookshops. Fear was added to my list of troubles, the fear of contracting a sexually transmitted disease.

I survived. I lied. I denied. I cried. I raged. I prayed. Oh, how I prayed! I did whatever it took to get through the tough moments to those times when I could close my eyes and my feelings to what was going on around me. The worst part was feeling Todd's hatred of me and of all women. He was punishing me for the sins of his mother, as if women were supposed to be perfect somehow. We weren't. We aren't. Gradually, I began to realize that if my life was ever to improve, I would have to be the one to change. I struggled to reach out and reach in, to find the woman who *I* was, the woman who had been lost years before. Since high school days in the late sixties, when female pastors were practically unheard of, I had longed to become an ordained minister myself. When I told the family I wanted to go to seminary, surprisingly, Todd and the kids encouraged me to take the plunge. In my late thirties I enrolled in one 250 miles from my home. Weekdays I lived in a seminary dorm; weekends I drove home.

Seminary became my drug. I thrived on the intellectual stimulation. My passions were stirred—for reading, for learning, for participating in intense intellectual relationships. My yearning for life, for justice, for love, for wholeness consumed me. In this place I was away from the one who sought to cage and own me, the one who abandoned me daily in his dalliances with other women, the one who unmercifully criticized my being, who verbally, sexually, and emotionally abused me with no remorse. And at seminary I fell in love.

I met Professor Jeff Jerkins my first week of classes. He was intelligent. He was intense. He was gorgeous. He was sensitive. His passion for justice, for righteousness, for liberation, all born out of his experiences of growing up African American in white America, drew me to him like a magnet.

Over the next year and a half, I came to admire and respect Jeff. Our paths seldom crossed, but when they did, the electricity between us crackled. During my middler year I enrolled in one of his classes. Now I had reason to go to his office. There we engaged in intense, deeply intellectual conversations and sparring matches that appeared to feed us both. Spirituality was at the heart of our conversations. We were both convinced of God's calling to work for justice: racial justice, gender justice, socioeconomic justice. The more engrossed I became with him, the less I wanted to go home to Todd.

Gradually I came to believe that Jeff was someone I could trust. He had ample opportunity to take advantage of me but chose not to, not then. He showed me respect, something to which I was unaccustomed. Most important, he appeared to like the person I was. The very things Todd abhorred in me—strength, intelligence, ambition, and more—were the things Jeff seemingly admired.

Enrolled as a full-time student, I also served as an associate pastor to three rural churches and as a part-time chaplain in a regional hospital some distance from the seminary. I worked on several seminary committees, and in the midst of all this, I continued to commute home every weekend. I was also trying to parent my children, all three of them in their teens by then. I was putting more than six hundred miles a week on the car.

Workaholism had taken hold of me. Many a night I cried myself to sleep, swearing I would slow down and end the madness, but I could not stop the frenetic behavior of my own free will. My judgment was impaired. My reasoning became illogical and irrational. Boundaries were skewed. Physically I was a wreck. I began to abuse alcohol, drinking in private every night before going to bed. I felt no pain. Up to this point, I had not talked to anyone about my marital difficulties. But it was only a matter of time before the dam burst.

Although I could not identify my feelings at the time, I now realize that pain, shame, rage, and resentment were seething beneath the surface. Jeff was there to catch me when I fell. In him I believed I had found someone who appreciated me for the person I was, someone who would understand the pain and oppression with which I had lived most of my life. In fact, Jeff often equated racial oppression with gender oppression, an equation which he suggested provided common ground for our relationship. As my friendship with Jeff grew, my feelings for Todd seemed to die, and I found it harder to forgive Todd's behavior.

Jeff began to share with me bits and pieces of his story, also a story of pain and abandonment. And he began to tell me of his affection for me—feelings he wasn't sure how to handle but would certainly guard so as not to hurt me. I was too valuable a friend to him—so he said. I was still naive enough to think we were talking about friendship at the deepest and most caring level.

In the summer between my middler and senior years, Jeff recommended me to Witness for Peace, to be part of a delegation to Nicaragua. Participants were to learn of Nicaraguans' struggles and return to the United States to press for changes in our country's policies toward Central America. Shortly before the trip I called him to talk. He had encouraged me for more than two years to share the heavy burden I carried and had expressed his willingness to be the counselor I needed. I thought he was safe. He was a friend, a confidant, a compassionate man who truly cared about my well-being. Surely he could be trusted with the secrets of my marriage.

That evening we drove to a nearby lake and walked out to the end of a pier, where I talked and talked and talked. He patiently listened, at times reaching over and gently touching my shoulder or squeezing my hand. When we walked back to his car, he made no inappropriate moves or comments. Finally I had found a man who was as good as his word.

Upon my return from Nicaragua in early October, Jeff invited me to his apartment to talk about my trip. I gladly accepted. That night I shared in detail the events of the previous weeks. In contrast, Todd never wanted to listen, never wanted to know, never mentioned the trip, never looked at my slides. By the end of the evening, Jeff was holding me in his arms as I talked and laughed with him. It had been so long since I had laughed. But I suddenly felt very uncomfortable and suggested it was time for me to leave. I couldn't tell him of the feelings stirring within me, feelings for him. What would he think of me if I were to cross boundaries? I told myself he was being a very pastoral, caring person and that I needed to leave before I did something stupid that might ruin a wonderful friendship.

From that point on, however, and at Jeff's urging, our relationship progressed rapidly. In my loneliness and intense desire to be loved, I must have seemed like putty in his hands. The affair was intense, thrilling, and short-lived. By Thanksgiving it was pretty much over. The ending was murky. Jeff simply drifted away, leaving subtle hints that he was no longer interested in being my "friend." But I couldn't let go. I tried to resurrect the romance in every way possible. I was once again accepting full responsibility for the failure of a relationship. Jeff's abandonment seemed to confirm that I truly was a failure as a woman and as a lover. Feelings of self-doubt and self-loathing overwhelmed me. The holidays were a nightmare.

Spring semester that year is a blur in my memory. I moved off campus, into an apartment away from the leering eyes and eavesdropping neighbors in the dorm. My apartment became for me a place of safety, my cocoon. Except for classes and work, I rarely ventured from it. The one pleasure I allowed myself was to join a health spa, but even that became an obsession. Each morning I religiously went to the gym, where workouts became frenetic endeavors to block out the pain. I shut down, did my work, shed forty pounds, and tried to commit suicide. I loathed myself. To this day I cannot remember sequentially what happened during that time. Occasionally I would run into Jeff. I would smile, act as if all were well, then continue on my way. But I was dying and disappearing as the weight continued to roll off. My friends were worried. They didn't know what was happening, and most kept their distance. They didn't know what to say or do for me.

That June, Jeff called and we went to the beach together. There was no spark, no interest, just emptiness and enormous pain and guilt. As usual, I smiled and pretended my way through the afternoon.

Not long afterward, while at an outdoor concert with seminary friends, the gossip turned to professors. Through this conversation I learned of Jeff's exploits with other students. I froze. Only then did I realize the magnitude of what had happened between us. His relationship with me had been a pattern, not some isolated incident, not an aberration in judgment (his), not an indictment against me, not a statement on my womanliness. I had been duped. Jeff had used me for his gratification just as Todd had used other women throughout our marriage.

I became enraged. I had unwittingly jumped from the bed of one addict into that of another. These two men were experts at using their charm and charisma—coupled with the power of their position and ordination—to seduce unsuspecting and hurting women, then to abandon them and pursue others. Neither man had a conscience or a sense of the depth of pain incurred by those who so desperately sought his counsel, his respect, his guidance, his love. Women had to be warned. But how?

In addition to the issues surrounding the misuse of power, there was the issue of race. (In my recovery I still have not adequately dealt with the ramifications of Jeff's being African American and my being white.) After careful consideration I decided that what had happened between us was a misuse of his power, regardless of race. This man had abused his position as minister, professor, and counselor to seduce women—African American and white—in their weakest moments, moments when they were seeking help. I had to speak. It would be hard, and the fallout would surely be painful. But could it be worse than what I had already endured? I naively thought that by making Jeff's and my relationship public, by seeking healing and justice from those in position to pass judgment, I would be "saving" womankind *and* redeeming myself. I was so wrong.

Finally I opened up to my closest friends, sharing with them the events of the past year and the pain I had endured, though without mentioning Todd's abuse. In the process, the names of some of Jeff's other victims surfaced. Cavalierly I chose to take official action, hoping others would join me in speaking out. They did not. No doubt they understood better than I the personal cost of making allegations.

My next step was to inform Todd, the children, and my church superiors of what had happened and of the possibility of a public scandal. Todd declared his undying love and forgiveness, promising to stand beside me through the ordeal. The children, although shocked that their mother was capable of such behavior, seemed relieved to know what had been causing the recent strange behavior and tension in our household. They, too, offered support, forgiveness, and unconditional love.

The church was another matter. Those high in the hierarchy cautioned me, "Don't be angry." My district supervisor warned me that whatever I chose to do I should do with the sole purpose of "rescuing Jeff." Without clarifying what he meant by that, he encouraged me to speak with our bishop.

The meeting with the bishop left me bewildered. His first words expressed relief that the disclosure did not involve his good friend, another pastor in the city where I was attending seminary. Maintaining a patronizing pastoral tone throughout the meeting, in essence he informed me that the church would do nothing.

Todd had accompanied me to the bishop's office, ostensibly to tell about his history of philandering and thus to put the matter into context. Instead, he spoke of his love for me and his forgiveness toward me, which I interpreted as a manipulative move to win favor with the bishop.

After these meetings I realized that the church was choosing to ignore the entire episode and encouraging me to do the same. "Fury" is the only word I know to describe my emotions at that time.

I entered my final semester of seminary. I vacillated between intense feelings of guilt and remorse over what I was doing to Jeff and feelings of personal power derived from finally standing up for myself and demanding a just response to an unjust situation. The vacillation, however, clouded my judgment. I doubted every move I made.

At one point I created a ritual, with the hope of breaking Jeff's spell over me. I wrote down things he had said and done, his endearing words and actions, as well as the cruel behavior and abandonment. I then burned the paper as I prayed, calling to myself the strength of my female ancestors who themselves had endured abuses in their lives. I summoned their strength to help me stand strong and firm in this mission I had undertaken. I then took the ashes, drove to the lake, and walked toward the end of the pier. A storm was raging. The waves pounded against the pier and washed over my feet; the wind whipped my jacket. I leaned into the wind for fear of being blown into the stormy waters. When I reached the end of the pier, I called on the powers of the four directions—shouting to hear myself—and claimed back the power I had relinquished to Jeff when I had first told him my story on that pier. I then threw the ashes to the wind, out onto the turbulent waters, releasing myself from that which bound me to Jeff. Walking back to my car, I experienced the first peace I had felt in months. While my ordeal was far from over, this ritual was crucial in my journey toward healing.

Not long afterward I filed an official complaint with the seminary. The first step was to write a complaint to the Title IX officer. Jeff was then allowed to respond in kind. He readily admitted to an affair, claiming his own vulnerability while simultaneously suggesting that it was my fault for having trusted him. He ended his response by stating that he had cared for me in our short time together and wished me well.

Though the guidelines for registering a complaint called for committee action within a specified amount of time, I had no indication that such action was taking place. One day when I stopped by her office to inquire what was being done, the Title IX officer suggested that I had filed the complaint only because Jeff had "dumped" me. Not once did she acknowledge the power differential and official policies against such behavior.

When I appeared before the committee to review my complaint—a committee of Jeff's peers and two of his students—the members expressed anger that I would not accept their decision that ours had been a mutual relationship. They, too, claimed I was merely acting the jilted lover. When the committee submitted its recommendations to the president of the seminary, he placed Jeff on one year's probation (a year in which Jeff was given a sabbatical) and agreed to pay for six counseling sessions for me. After one year Jeff's record was to be purged so this incident would not follow him around for the rest of his career. To my knowledge, nothing else was done.

At school I was vilified as the seducer of the "vulnerable professor." In the church I was the one who had abandoned Todd, the devoted husband and father, the beloved pastor. For several months I was threatened via anonymous phone calls two and three times a day: sometimes silence hung on the other end of the line; at other times I was warned to be silent, to watch my back, not to make waves if I wanted to graduate. Peers with whom I had worked and studied for years shunned me. Family members who knew the story remained silent or expressed sympathy and support for Todd for enduring my "crusade." I went for days without sleeping. I lived on coffee and chips and salsa. To make things worse, the bishop had no job appointment for me. My district supervisor never again spoke to me of the issue or asked how I was faring. To this day the church has not addressed the issue with me.

As graduation approached, a professor sought to bribe me into skipping the ceremony and accepting my diploma in absentia. At a pregraduation service, Jeff was asked to be the clergy to serve communion to the graduating seniors. While I did not attend that service, I chose to go through the graduation ceremony, thus forcing the ones who would silence me and make me invisible to hand me my diploma and to place the hood on my shoulders. My colleagues in ministry, for the most part, ignored me. These ministers of the gospel spoke no words of comfort or support. Throughout the ordeal I found that my strongest support and care came primarily from people outside the church.

Just weeks after graduation I suffered a complete collapse and was admitted to a treatment center in the Southwest. I spent two months in rehab that summer, gaining the tools to begin healing from a lifetime of deep wounds at the hands of those who claimed to love me. It was in that setting that I began to learn how to identify and reclaim my feelings, communicate my needs, take care of myself, and establish functional boundaries.

I still struggled with the marriage. Todd and I had to declare bankruptcy because of his uncontrollable spending and my inability to get work. Sexually I shut down. I would not allow anyone, especially my husband, to touch me. Nonetheless, after treatment I returned home to Todd with renewed hope for a better life and for healing. He, too, had gone through extensive counseling and treatment during the previous two years. It was my belief that we now had the tools and the desire to save our marriage, to repair the brokenness. I envisioned a new relationship based on respect, mutuality, and forgiveness.

The next two years were not easy. We struggled with what it meant to relate to each other in new ways. Healing the wounds of emotional and sexual abuse was difficult at best. I continued in therapy.

As I became stronger, I began to demand equality in our decision-making processes, something new in our relationship. Our next geographic move was my call—the first time in twenty-four years that I had had a say in where we were to live. I accepted a pastoral appointment, with Todd's support, to a rural parish in another state, with the understanding that when he had completed his contract at the hospital where he was chaplain, he would join me, and we would continue in a new life together. That never happened.

Todd entered into an affair with a nurse at the hospital. On the day she filed for divorce, he told me he wanted one too. The pain of this final betrayal cut me to the core. In spite of our history, I had allowed myself to believe that we could have a happy future together. Hadn't we both been in therapy? Hadn't we both acquired new skills for mending our relationship? Now there could be no more denials, no more naïveté. I finally understood that I could not save the marriage and that Todd and I would have to go our separate ways.

But not before the loathing and hatred I felt toward myself erupted in one final act of volcanic proportions. In a fit of pain and rage, I one night drank myself into oblivion, trashed Todd's apartment, and slashed my body with broken glass and razors. The effects of twenty-five years of abuse came pouring out. I cut this body of mine because of the overwhelming sorrow that if I had only been prettier or smarter, kinder or more understanding, Todd would have been able to love me. I wanted to see my pain, not just feel it. I wanted the church to see my blood and to know how deeply I hurt. I wanted Todd to feel remorse, to feel *anything.*

This ritual, this self-mutilation, was the result of a lifetime of clergy sexual abuse. The church had long ignored my pain. The seminary had sought to silence me. Everyone wanted me to be invisible. I had been held responsible for the success or failure of my marriage and had yet to hear anyone address Todd's behavior, especially as it pertained to his roles as husband and pastor. In fact, to this day I can name ordained ministers in our conference who continue to collude with him in his affairs, supporting his behavior by word and deed, encouraging him to rid himself of me.

My self-mutilation, born of intense pain and self-loathing, bought me a week's stay in the psychiatric unit of the hospital where Todd was chaplain. But not until I had lain drunk in a pool of my own blood for the entire night. Todd, not wanting his professional reputation sullied, did not call 911 when he found me, nor did he get me to the hospital until he could make arrangements the next day to do so discreetly with the help of some of his friends. This incident, which so clearly demonstrated his lack of love, broke Todd's hold on me. Finally I realized, without a doubt, that maintaining the persona of the gentle, caring chaplain was more important to him than my life, that indeed he would rather I die than that people know the truth of our marriage.

Since that day, Todd's credentials as an ordained minister have been revoked by the denomination. However, he continues to work as a hospital chaplain. The church, while it has revoked his credentials, has never offered a word of comfort or support to me. I remain on leave of absence from parish ministry as I struggle with the decision of whether to remain in a church that seems unable to come to grips with the devastating effects of clergy sexual misconduct on *all* parties involved. Spiritually speaking, the church has little to offer in the way of healing and wholeness. I am finding healing in other places, in other ways, with other people.

As I write these words, the divorce is finally taking place. People ask me why I stayed in the marriage so long. Besides my religious beliefs, which were strong chains, I stayed because there were brief moments of joy, glimpses of hope that made me think life could be different and better. Even now I picture the two of us romantically dancing around a campfire while the children slept. I remember Todd's presence and active involvement at the birth of each of our children. I smile at the memory of skinny-dipping in the ocean at the break of day and intimate walks in the evening. And there were his repeated displays of remorse and vows to change. He gave me unexpected gifts and wrote poetry and songs, all expressing undying, unending love. He was the ultimate charmer, and I wanted to be charmed. I wanted to believe his words long after I knew how empty they were. But these expressions of love were few and far between. Our lives were dominated by his obsession with other women and sex, and by my distorted belief that I could save him from himself by denying *my self, my* needs, *my* desires.

There is more to this story. I am only now discovering the value of making my voice heard, my presence seen, my tears felt. I have come to realize that I do not have to carry the secrets around with me. This does not mean that I reveal all the details of my life to everyone I meet. Rather, speaking out has made it possible for me to address the abuse for myself, to look at my issues and my own complicity—to clean house. Whether or not the other players in this saga chose to use the situation for their own healing and transformation, I did. Today I am a different woman, a stronger woman, a healthier woman for having made my voice heard. I no longer have to carry around the shame. In that sense I am a free woman for having spoken.

Through the course of events, I also discovered indomitable strength. Not until I confronted Jeff, the seminary, the church,

Todd, and others did I begin to grasp the depth of pain that so many women before me have endured. Now I realize that I can indeed make choices for myself—for health, for wholeness, for justice. I consciously *chose* to survive, and then, once I knew I would, I *chose* to continue along the path of healing to a place of thriving. I very much like being a woman standing in her strength.

The story of Jesus healing the bent-over woman (Luke 13:10–17) is now my story. The woman had been bent over for decades. No one told her she could stand up straight and tall until she encountered Jesus. When she stood up, the church leaders were paralyzed. How could Jesus do such a thing? Yet he had only spoken the word; she was the one who stood up! But the holy men wouldn't even address their concerns directly to the woman who now stood among them. There was no celebration, only berating for her standing up. But stand she did! I, too, now stand up straight. And I like the person I have become.

Strangely, I find that my anger toward Todd and Jeff is tinged with sorrow over events in their lives that compel (and support) them to perpetrate evil upon unsuspecting victims. The real rage I feel is directed more toward the institutions and the players within those institutions who fight so tenaciously to maintain the status quo, even though they speak words to the contrary. When one of their own is exposed, rather than open doors to healing for all concerned, church leaders often close ranks around the perpetrator and seek to silence the messenger.

Church leaders and seminary administrators could have taken steps to prevent Todd and Jeff from abusing again. Those in power could have required rigorous supervision and could have insisted on accountability and restitution. They could have provided support for me through counseling and by upholding their own policies. In that way an environment of safety would have been created for others seeking healing from abuse. Such actions would have been steps toward redeeming an unjust situation. Instead, their decision not to act but to protect their own and to hush up the incidents superseded any notion of redemption. Thus, more injustice was inflicted, a great deal more.

I now work with incarcerated women as a counselor and educator. I have become outspoken on issues of abuse and often find myself advocating for women who suffer at the hands of those in positions of authority. One of the unexpected surprises for me is the respect I now receive from other women. It never occurred to me, in the midst of the mud and muck, that other women, most of them not even knowing my story, would see me as a leader or look to me as some sort of an example. I am still baffled by this. I am realizing for the first time that meaning can be wrought from adversity, strength from suffering, and that somehow we victims can indeed be transformed by this whole process—if we choose—into light for others who have yet to experience their own transformations.

Throughout the process of surviving, I chose to find redemption for myself in many ways. As a result, to me, justice has come to mean living with integrity and making choices not to abuse, not to act in vengeful ways, and not to become bitter with the living of life. Even more, justice means to be aware of who I am, how I relate, and how I will make choices to enhance life rather than deny life. I now use the term "redemptive justice" when I consider how to make meaning of the evil we women encounter, how to find relief in an unjust situation, or how to heal from the pain of injustice. I also use this term as I consider my own unjust actions and my need to be accountable for my choices. I, too, have had to make amends for having no boundaries and for allowing my life to spin out of control. That act of recognizing and owning my part in this story is part of my reclaiming my power, of moving from victim, which I was, to victor, which I now am.

More than ever, I am convinced that all people are called to a life of service. This means not menial servitude but service to practice goodness in the face of evil, to speak when told to be silent, to stand when told to sit (or vice versa), to do what we can to alleviate suffering, live with integrity, and walk upright without shame. Living such a life does make a difference. I know that now.

Each day, as I continue to integrate the events of my life and to make meaning out of those events, I become increasingly grateful for the life I have been given. I am profoundly moved as I realize the depth of love and friendship I have experienced from those few who have walked this journey by my side. I am compelled to offer the same friendship to others I encounter as they walk through their fires. I share the lessons I have learned, knowing without a doubt that women were never meant to be bent over. In fact, bent-over women will continue to stand up straight and to make their voices heard. And that is biblical!

If someone were to ask me today, "Would you do it all over again?"—referring to my making the official complaint against Jeff—I would answer with a resounding "Yes!" In spite of the grief and pain endured in an evil system, I would do it all again, because through it all I have been freed from that which bent me over. Speaking out opened the door to healing, to love and compassion, and to mercy and forgiveness for myself and ultimately for others.

CHAPTER TWO

Repairing the Damage
of a Shepherd
ET AL

When I say the Lord's Prayer, I am overcome by pain and stumble over the word "father." I beg God for answers to the question of why I was damaged. I question the scriptures that interpret suffering as punishment, then wonder what sin I must be atoning for. Where is the miracle to replace the carnage of my life?

I have existed for almost five decades in a world that has generally been unkind. I fought for much of what I have. I was born in a small town where my extended family included the whole neighborhood. People knew of my father's drinking and physically abusive behavior, but no one intervened or said his actions were wrong.

Since my father's paycheck supported the family, Mama tolerated his verbal and physical abuse. She coped by trying to ignore it and sought comfort in reading Scripture or listening to the radio evangelist extol the redemptive power of suffering. She accepted the notion that my father's drinking on weekends was her cross to bear.

In the summer of 1951, I was the only black child in my hometown to get polio. I was never healed, though my mother and I prayed faithfully. The churches we attended talked about a punishing God who sent tribulations and plagues to the Israelites to make them repent for their sins or as retribution for the sins of their fathers. The radio evangelists said healing occurred if one believed in God's power. When the polio didn't go away, I concluded that Mama's and my faith wasn't strong enough.

Since people didn't do much about Daddy's physical abuse, I never told anyone about the sexual abuse he inflicted. I accepted the burden for being mistreated, believing that my polio and the accompanying financial problems justified his behavior.

Mama's death shortly before I turned fourteen led to a crisis in faith. My father's sexual abuse increased, but I never told anyone except God. God didn't seem to be listening, though. Less than six months after Mama's death, my father, who was now drinking almost all the time, lost his job. He never again provided any financial support for us. My brothers, age nineteen and seventeen, got jobs to support me and my sister, who was ten. At about that time I began to think of my father by his first name, Henry, because I didn't see his abusive actions as fatherly.

Angry with God about Mama's death, I no longer wanted to be part of a religion that would allow children to struggle alone. I quit going to church. In our small town everyone knew that Henry was drinking all the time and that he wasn't living with us. Some of the church family were teachers who saw our daily struggle yet offered only limited support. When I quit attending church, no one came by the house to ask why. My anger and subsequent rebellion against religion lasted almost three years.

In my senior year of high school, I began to search for a church family to replace my biological one. I knew that as soon as I graduated, my sister would go to live with one brother who had moved to another state for employment. Since I could find no solace in the church in which I had been baptized or in the churches of my friends, I reconnected with God through one in which I had no family or cultural ties.

I learned the tenets of my new faith from Patrick, a priest. For five months I studied with him weekly, telling him many of my secrets. I told him about the emotional pain of going to the welfare department to get food subsidies. I described my agony at being responsible for my father's going to jail for not paying child support. I explained that Henry's family blamed me for his imprisonment and for his drinking. I never mentioned the worst secret, the sexual abuse. Patrick, who didn't approve of my anger toward Henry, told me to confess those things that would be a barrier to my being a good child of God.

But Patrick also knew my dreams for the future and encouraged me in school. He attended my graduation from high school; my father did not.

I went to college twelve miles from my hometown. College took its toll on my self-esteem. I had been the valedictorian of a small black high school but had had limited exposure to the chemistry and biology that classmates from metropolitan areas took for granted. I managed to receive accolades but secretly believed I was inferior. My financial support was limited, so I had the extra pressure of maintaining the scholarships I had received.

I was also lonely. Some weekends I visited my maternal aunt's home but spent most of the time defending my decision to change churches. I was questioned about the mostly white congregation and ridiculed for fasting before going to communion.

I sought respite and support in talks with Patrick. He encouraged me to stay away from people who didn't belong to my adopted religion and urged me to keep my new beliefs. I began to find rides from college to the Sunday service so I wouldn't have to spend weekends with relatives.

When I was nineteen and a sophomore in college, my father died. The years of suppressed rage at his abuse erupted, and I decided not to attend his funeral. Even when I told Patrick how my father had sexually abused me, he seemed disappointed in me and insisted I go. "Honor your father and mother," he reminded me. "Forgive and forget." He also discouraged me from discussing the painful secrets with anyone but him. Fearing Patrick's disapproval, I went to my father's funeral.

Patrick's admonition to forget reinforced the many years I had managed my life by dissociating. Dissociation is a coping skill I learned as a child so I wouldn't remember the abuse I endured. It is a defense mechanism similar to veterans' suppression of the ravages of war with shell shock, or post-traumatic stress disorder. As a child I discovered how not to exist in my body while being physically or sexually abused. I daydreamed that the events were happening to someone else. This other person held the memory and rarely talked about the trauma. Over time, by becoming many people in this way, I could handle the pain of abuse. Part of me could forget the horror.

Following my father's death I was confused, and I turned to Patrick for counsel. Looking back, I see that that's when he began to exploit my vulnerability. He was interested in the sexual details of incest but didn't want to hear about the shame I felt. He minimized the destructiveness of my father's abuse, linking it to drinking. Now, thirty years later, I recall that Patrick began to give me prolonged hugs, supposedly to comfort me when I cried about the pain of incest. He patted my leg when I told him about being bewildered by my father's touch during my hospitalization with polio.

My spiritual leader began setting our appointments when no one else was around the rectory. The door and patio drapes closed, he removed his clerical collar—claiming he could relax around me—then gave me sacramental wine to ease my discomfort over discussing my past abuse.

With trusting innocence, I turned to him for advice when I entered delayed puberty. It was the summer before my junior year of college, and I didn't understand my sexual stirrings and interest in a classmate. The uneasy feelings and fantasies sent me running to my "father figure." He warned me of the danger and chance of sinfulness if I told this secret to the classmate I idolized from afar. He listened to my naive report of self-touching, which I didn't learn until years later was called masturbation. My pastor/counselor encouraged me to tell him the fantasies and suggested I act out my curiosity with him in the safety of the pastor's office or the rectory living room. Sitting close to me, he told me I needed to express the sexual feelings in a safe place, with him. He began to kiss me, laughing at my inexperience when I didn't know what to do with his tongue in my mouth. He quieted any opposition with the assertion that he knew what was best for me.

During later appointments, he showed me things to avoid with boys if I wanted to be a good Christian girl. Without asking any questions, I dutifully did as he suggested. All the while I survived in the only way I knew: I dissociated and didn't remember what happened in the house next to God's house. I was an expert at forgetting and keeping quiet. I didn't even tell God what was being done to me.

In my senior year of college, I abandoned fantasies about my classmate and became withdrawn and depressed. I went to my family doctor, because I was concerned about my erratic menstrual cycle. I expected him to tell me it was related to the polio of my childhood, but instead he told me I was pregnant. I told him he was wrong; I wasn't dating anyone. Because of my dissociation, I had no conscious knowledge of intercourse with my "spiritual father." When a second test in the doctor's office showed I was pregnant, he recommended that I be tested at the hospital. Patrick took me to the hospital for the third test, which found I was not pregnant. That night I attempted suicide and had to go to the emergency room to have my stomach pumped. Instead of discussing my depression, Patrick informed me that suicide was a mortal sin that would prevent my Christian burial.

My erratic stability became noticeable as my senior year of college continued. I was terrified about graduating and possibly taking a job away from Patrick. I became more suicidal and finally requested hospitalization when my attempt at self-asphyxiation endangered someone else's life. I spent six months on a psychiatric ward. In all that time I never discussed the years of incest. And of course, having no consciousness of Patrick's abuse, I said nothing about that, either. I gave the social worker only a limited family history, so all she knew was that I was an orphan struggling financially to complete college. The doctor identified the problem as low self-esteem.

My one regular visitor was Patrick, who discussed my history with the social worker but did not, to my knowledge, ever tell her about my having grown up in a home filled with domestic violence and alcoholism. I wonder today if he was there to make sure I said nothing about our relationship.

I returned to complete my last year of college, but all my friends had graduated in May. On his days off duty, Patrick usually took me along to rectories of other priests, presenting me as his "special friend." He and the others gave me liquor, though according to state drinking laws, I was underage. On one occasion we attended a St. Patrick's Day party along with three other Irish priests and two nursing students who had just arrived from Ireland. One of the priests recited raunchy limericks, and the music was turned up to drown out cries from the bedroom. No one seemed to wonder why I, a young black woman, was taking part in their cultural event.

I was devastated when, several months before my graduation, Patrick was transferred to a new parish in the same state. After the church's farewell party, he asked me to accompany him back to the rectory. There, in a "secret ceremony," he gave me a blessed medal and placed it around my neck. This symbolized his love for me and meant we would be together in heaven, he said. I was to tell no one about our spiritual relationship. The medal was broken that night in rough sexual activity. Patrick moved the next day.

Even the sense of accomplishment that came with graduating from college, getting a professional job, then going on to finish a graduate degree in social work did not alleviate the overwhelming sadness I felt in the ensuing years. The degrees only added to my feelings of despair. Someone so successful would dare not disclose dirty family secrets. Stays at psychiatric hospitals and countless hours of therapy made no sense to people who saw me as a competent social worker. I was seen as a role model, a professional black woman living the American dream.

My family and friends saw me as high-strung. I never told them about a past that made me feel unworthy of their love and kindness. Believing I was not supposed to marry, I never cultivated long-standing relationships with men. After all, I was going to be with Patrick in heaven.

To maintain appearances, I never told my therapists of the shame that tormented me at night. Turning my anger inward, I tried to damage or destroy my body. I swallowed caustic liquids to keep myself from speaking the truth. I set my body on fire to punish it for the guilt and shame it caused me. At that time I didn't realize I was using the coping mechanisms of dissociation. Part of me had no conscious knowledge of the years of abuse.

There were two more psychiatric hospitalizations, both after I'd been to visit Patrick in his new parish. My direct contact with him did not end until I left the area at the age of thirty-two to take a job as a social worker more than a thousand miles away.

When I had been relocated only two months, a friend died tragically. I searched for a new church home and found a congregation that accepted me as part of the family. I became active on committees and in religious education programs. When I began again to experience the recurring depression, the pastor of my new church referred me to a competent psychologist.

For the first time I revealed to a therapist the abuse I had suffered as a child. Perhaps I was finally able to talk about it because, as a social worker, I was exposed to cases of child abuse and knew its damage. My therapist gave me a gift that saved my life: he told me I was not responsible for Henry's incest or physical abuse. In all those years no one had told me that. The years of secrecy, guilt, and shame began to crumble.

With the revelation of my father's sexual abuse, it became possible to more accurately diagnose my underlying psychological problem as multiple personality disorder. I learned that my dissociating from trauma was my way of coping with the abuse of childhood. I had developed various personalities to handle the violence and swallow the anger yet to perform well academically and professionally.

The difficult task of therapy—to heal from the abuse—took its toll on my everyday life. Recovery from past abuse and movement toward an integration of my personalities was uneven. My long-submerged anger began to surface, and I became fearful of bringing harm to someone. To prevent my inadvertently doing anything detrimental to my patients, I decided to file for disability. It was granted because of my multiplicity. I cut back on my church activities, especially those involving children. In 1986, because of the intense pain that came with remembering the incest and abuse, my psychologist ordered thirty days of psychiatric hospitalization to monitor my behavior and prevent suicide.

The following year, I returned to my former pattern of denying the abuse. I needed external proof of the childhood trauma. I contacted one of my brothers, who verified to my therapist by phone his knowledge of the physical violence in our family. He stated that though he hadn't been told about the sexual abuse, he believed I was telling the truth. My therapist asked me if there was anyone else who might have known about the sexual abuse at a time close to the original trauma. I told him that Patrick had been my support for many years.

With my permission, the therapist contacted Patrick. A few sessions later, I revealed another secret: that Patrick's and my relationship had been sexual. This revelation prompted my therapist to insist that Patrick come to my next therapy sessions, which he reluctantly agreed to do.

As if he were the expert, Patrick dominated the two days of videotaped sessions. He said he had a vague memory of inconsequential touching but insisted it had been for my benefit and was a selfless action on his part. He vehemently denied intercourse. He acknowledged that he had been told of the incest but did not see it as important and had urged me to forget the events. During the sessions, whenever I mentioned the return of memories, Patrick changed the direction of the conversation or claimed to have forgotten the details. He gave rambling, confused accounts of my emotional state when I had gone to him for counseling. He admitted that he had sometimes ordered me to undress or go to his bedroom. He also recalled that I had often appeared dazed, yet he had chosen not to talk with me about what had happened in the rectory. He then reported a time when I had fondled him, not mentioning that he had taught me to touch him. Finally, as if on God's behalf, he said he forgave me for the harm I had done him.

Patrick left town after those two days, urging me to forget the "unfortunate memories" I was beginning to recover. Those days that he sat in my therapist's office clearly mark the time when I began to realize consciously the abusive nature of my relationship with him. The sessions, videotaped with his permission, are a visual account of his words and treatment. I have external proof of his behavior and arrogance. Periodically, when I begin to blame myself for Patrick's abuse, I view the tapes.

The therapy sessions with Patrick were the beginning of discovery. I saw that the dissociative skills that had helped me survive my biological father's abuse had also helped me survive the trauma of sexual abuse by my spiritual father. As I look back, I see that I became childlike in response to his authority. I developed more personalities to answer the horrid demands of a perpetrator who skillfully covered his actions by coercing my forgetfulness and ability to keep secrets.

Painfully piecing together my past brought forward crucial data about the suicide patterns. I realized I had made no suicidal attempts until Patrick made our relationship a sexual one. The cruel actions of my biological father had never pushed me to the depths of trying to end my life. The confusion over my spiritual father's conduct was the missing link to the puzzle of my ongoing death wish.

Then I began to have flashbacks while attending church. As memories returned, I was overcome by guilt over things that had taken place years before in church rectories. However, instead of holding Patrick accountable, I saw myself as responsible for sullying the actions of a priest and for therefore condemning other parishioners he served. Believing I would be punished for tainting God's servant, I felt unworthy to partake of communion and began to withdraw from church involvement. Strangely, I tried to reach Patrick for guidance about the flashbacks, but he didn't return my calls.

The struggle to find healing has been cyclical. I have had to search alone for hidden memories of things done in church rectories, offices, and bedrooms. The need to keep secrets caused me to block the trauma, often by creating another alter personality. The confusion over the behavior of one who assumed the responsibility to be a shepherd could not be contained in just one personality.

I recall being pulled over with Patrick along a dark roadside when a highway patrol officer could have protected me, but the clerical collar stopped any questions of impropriety. Alone I must try to remember the events that led to my being given sacramental wine before he sat next to me and touched my leg or taught me to French-kiss. Without other witnesses I must try to recollect the sounds coming from the bedroom at the party on St. Patrick's Day. I search to discover why certain days or objects, like medals, send me into the deepest depressions. I yearn for the peace of believing that God knows the truth and loves me anyway.

Therapy has helped toward building a healthy life. My most recent therapist had to transcend my constant caution about whether he could be trusted not to harm or abuse me. I have had to learn many lessons: that a person with power and access to my vulnerabilities can and will act ethically; that I can say no and set realistic boundaries for myself; that my openness and giving are positive qualities to be nourished; and perhaps the hardest, that recovery is an ongoing process with setbacks and stumbling blocks. Twice again I have had to be hospitalized when the pain of memories became too great.

As I EXPLORED THE DESTRUCTIVE NATURE of my relationship with Patrick, I needed to take steps to move me away from the role of victim. I wanted to become a survivor, a woman who trusted her own understanding of what had happened to her, a woman who took action. Searching for earthly justice and—given that I was barely making it on my disability income—compensation to pay the mounting cost of professional therapy, I decided to file a civil lawsuit. I wanted a jury of peers to verify that I had been wronged. I wanted to stop the actions of an abuser still functioning as a pastor. The fact that Patrick had shown no signs of true remorse made me wonder what harm he might be doing others. I requested a day in court to prove my facts.

My belief in the church and its congregants has been terribly shaken by the response to my filing legal charges. Instead of dealing with the truth of my accusations, the church's and Patrick's lawyers chose to bar my suit because of the statute of limitations. Their argument was that I had recovered the memory and degree of the abusive behavior too late. During a four-year legal struggle, the bishops did not respond to me or to the abuse described in the court documents.

As the legal battles wore on, I decided to picket outside the church Patrick served. I did this to demonstrate my concerns about the continuing harmful capabilities of my abuser. When two friends and I tried to distribute a fact sheet about my charges, parishioners called the police. The administrative offices of the diocese were locked the next day when a longtime friend and I quietly picketed again. In subsequent news coverage, journalists interviewed only representatives for the church and Patrick. The morning newspaper reported that the church had decided not to investigate my claims, because I had mental problems.

The church's legal counsel successfully blocked my day in court.

The lack of concern by the organized church for me and my spiritual welfare has remained a constant heartache. No Christlike compassion was shown as my recovery of the buried abuse took me close to death. I frequently struggle with why I should remain in a religious body that shows a callous disregard for members who are harmed by those in leadership roles.

MY JOURNEY FROM BEING A VICTIM to being a survivor has taken me through stages similar to the ones described by Elisabeth Kübler-Ross in her book *On Death and Dying.* These divisions help give boundaries to the rampant and often fluid emotions I have experienced in my healing.

Of the five stages, I appear to have spent the most time in the first phase, denial. For most of the fifteen years I was involved with Patrick, I never saw that his actions were damaging. I naively believed he cared about my well-being and, most of all, about my soul. I saw him as trustworthy and thought he could do no wrong, as he was a representative of God. Denial was such a strong coping pattern that it took hours of therapy to see his abusive actions for what they were.

On the other hand, my denial enabled me to exist. Because I falsely believed I had the support of a spiritual father, I was able to complete college and graduate school. Denial also slowed down the recurring pain as my memory began to uncover Patrick's confusing actions. There may still be unrecovered facts that I am unable to handle emotionally at present, so I allow them to remain a hidden secret.

Depression, Kübler-Ross's second stage in dealing with death, engulfs my life. In my fifty years of living, I don't remember many days when the melancholia hasn't been there. For most of those years, I had no explanation for the debasement I felt or for the belief that I was being punished by God. I was unable to accept positive feedback from others; their affirmation could not balance the unspoken secrets. I now know the antecedent of the low self-esteem, but I don't always know the triggers of pain that push me to the brink of self-destruction. Professional therapy gave me new tools with which to decrease the suicidal attempts, but I still must work to control self-abusive behavior.

Anger, Kübler-Ross's third stage, has become my lifeline to sanity. My recovery process has helped me see that anger is an acceptable feeling, that it has in fact been part of me all along. It quietly fueled a belief that I had the right to be alive and not to be mistreated by anyone. I could write volumes about my anger at Patrick, at the bishops, at the legal system, and at others who have chosen to protect and shelter an abusive priest.

Many people who have to hear anger are uneasy with the intense emotion. They want the volume turned down to a level that doesn't make them uncomfortable. They ignore the pain behind it, not understanding that the survivor did not have a voice or was not heard when the abuse was taking place.

Remembering and recovering have taught me to cherish my anger. It screams that I have been mistreated. My demand for kindness and humane treatment gives voice to a new understanding that I am a lovable, precious child of God. My anger says I choose not to let an abuser decide my self-worth and my connection to God.

I don't know which is worse, the original trauma or Patrick's refusal to accept responsibility for betraying my trust. It is difficult for me not to want vengeance when I remember the times I was ordered to undress and to lie next to him in the pastor's bed. My blood boils as I recall that he gave me sacramental wine before the mock ceremony bonding me to him. I seethe as I struggle to understand what trait of mine signaled that I would not challenge his authority. Did my race give him the assurance that my revelation of abuse would be ignored or disbelieved? My perpetual voicing of indignation is my quest for earthly justice.

Kübler-Ross's fourth stage, bargaining, has both transitory and permanent features for me. As a survivor of childhood abuse, I believed I deserved punishment for something bad I must have done. I had to have a cause-effect explanation because a sense of random abuse created panic. Needing to believe that mistreatment from others was within my control, I tried to bargain for good treatment by being obedient and helpful.

Knowing I had assumed the guilt and shame about the incest, Patrick exploited my desire to find acceptance and a loving father. I falsely believed that I had to allow the sexual incidents with Patrick in order to undo my badness. Otherwise, he would abandon me just as my biological father had.

In life I look for predictability. I barter for happiness by believing that my service to others can be redemptive. I still pray for validation that I did not deserve the abuse. I break the bonds of secrecy, hoping to give solace to another survivor experiencing the storm of desperation. I search for the loving family that will mirror my innate goodness. I battle for the inclusion rather than exclusion of survivors of clergy misconduct in all houses of worship. I barter for an elusive peace of mind by thanking God that I lived one more day. This phase of bargaining keeps me searching for an answer to my hellish life.

Acceptance, Kübler-Ross's last stage, eludes me the most. I don't have a clear definition of what is required for my well-being. Sometimes when I hear the word "acceptance," I assume that others want me to return to secreting away the pain and damage of clergy abuse. Why can't I just turn the experiences over to God and believe that God will solve the problem? If I accept anything, it is that I have a responsibility to help remove perpetrators from church positions where they have access to vulnerable people.

I take up residence in the acceptance phase when I avow my life experience. I am among the growing number of women who say we were abused at vulnerable times in our life. I voice the truth that I have been betrayed by people who were charged with my caretaking through the roles they assumed. I acknowledge that I survived catastrophic events by dissociating, as that was the best option at the time. I believe that I have survived, even with the scars and deep, bleeding wounds, because of internal strength, not weakness. I accept that not everyone can or will be helpful and supportive in my recovering process but that I indeed have a right to be whole and healed.

I choose to go forward, even when I take temporary steps backward. I choose to know the truth of the past mistreatment and assert that I did not deserve what happened to me. I now accept that I was betrayed and that my sacred trust was violated. I acknowledge that I need to continue to break the chains of secrecy if I am to foster my own healing and a belief in organized religion. Acceptance has its struggles, and I see as I continue recovering that it is part of all the other phases.

HEALING FROM ABUSE has been uneven and costly. While professional therapy with an ethical clinician was crucial, the most important resource has been the love I receive from those who want me to live and to find happiness.

My strongest support comes from a constant confidant, who helps me weather the day-to-day task of choosing to be a better representative of God. For those of us who have been abused, finding a trustworthy relationship is difficult. One that lasts is a cornerstone for growth.

I also rely on the support of other survivors. My own healing jumped by leaps and bounds when I realized I was not the only person victimized by someone dressed in religious garb. While I often live with self-blame, I do not blame the woman next to me for the situation that caused her pain. As we talk about our experi-

ences, we end years of isolation. The women in this unique family
had their trust betrayed, and many, like me, question belief in a
loving God. These new friends seldom give advice, and they are
patient in letting me share my experience at my own pace.

I also have found healing in very tangible ways. I have put the
truth on paper, generally in poetry but more recently in prose. In
therapy I drew pictures of the torture and raw distress. A picture
truly can be worth a thousand words. The drawings and collages
I kept are reminders that I have journeyed toward a reconnection
with my soul and a belief in a loving God.

I have found a way to release the pain locked in my body. I
schedule deep-muscle massage to reach the aches that are the resi-
due of the negative energy housed inside. Mentally releasing the
shame and guilt I carry, I try to see my body as good and valuable. I deserve soft, caring touch.

I find encouragement and support in the writings of others. I
have an extensive library. Reading about the struggles of others, I
find courage. I get tips from therapists I've never met, and for the
cost of their books I can access their support any time I need it.
Sometimes a book never gets opened; its title is all I need to keep
me journeying toward healing. I often find similarities in the recovery of survivors of various abuses. As I read their reports, I
wonder if there is an unknown training school that teaches perpetrators how to prey on the vulnerable.

WHEN I THINK OF HOW I've been denied the earthly justice I seek,
I experience trouble in my prayer life or in my ability to meditate.
I cherish the comforting words of my present pastor, who listens
to my questioning God's lack of mercy. My effort to affiliate
with an organized body of followers of Christ is tenuous and
uneven, and I certainly understand fellow survivors who have left
organized religion.

To maintain my sanity, I have become vocal about the evil of
clergy sexual misconduct. I view myself as an activist who chal-

lenges church bodies to live the exemplary virtues they extol. I am an agitator who refuses to allow dirty secrets to go unchallenged. I am a rebel who demands earthly accountability of church leaders. If I appear contentious, it is because of my experience that the squeaky wheel gets the oil. I battle to make church policies on clergy misconduct more than mere pieces of paper for legal protection. I speak out today because the silence and secrecy of abuse have taken the lives of victims who did not experience the support they wanted and needed in their journey toward healing.

There are days when I want to walk away from this battle. I keep searching for Christlike compassion, and I am thankful when I find support, as when ministers and church leaders genuinely apologize for the pain inflicted by others who wear a clerical collar.

Some days I choose to abandon formal religion. I gather peace in my journey by relying on the beauty and magnitude of nature. I relish the massiveness of the mountains and imagine the patience and loving care of my creator, who designed the masterpiece. I bask in the calm of a still day and am rejuvenated by a breeze or the song of a bird. I try to nurture the soul that was given me by God. These rest stops are the fuel that keeps me in a process of recovering. When I am able to separate the perpetrator and his supporters from the one I call Creator, I become reconnected with God.

"Dreaming" and "hoping" are difficult words for me. In my heart I know I have an important place in this universe. I also think this world was created with a planned orderliness, but it is hard for me to understand the chaos of my life. So I am in a process, continuously becoming.

I am better today not because of forgiving and forgetting but because of remembering and recovering. Survival is what I am about, and it is what I have tried to share in this account. I want other survivors of abuse to know they are not alone.

Stolen Not Lost
Et Al

I learned a valuable lesson today about responsibility.
I now know where to leave the shame and blame.
I am beginning to discover the truth—
Many of my precious gifts were stolen, not lost.

You stole my unquestioned belief in my creator's love;
You stole the preciousness of solitude in God's presence;
You stole the joy of coming together to share Eucharist;
You stole my reverence for the deep meaning of a church family;
You stole my ability to be quiet and hear God's voice;
You stole my belief in the phrase "God answers prayers";
You stole the joy I felt in calling myself Christian;
You stole my ability to find comfort in going to confession;
You stole my innocence and twisted my trust in humankind;
You stole my hope for a better tomorrow and instilled doubt;
You stole my love of life and wanting to live;
You stole my belief in the basic goodness of people;
You stole a significant part of my childhood and adolescence;
You stole my desire to become a loving adult woman;
You stole my voice and actions that screamed a loud NO;
You stole my right to claim my justifiable anger at abuse;
You stole my right to easily risk counsel without suspicion;
You stole the inner peace I experienced entering God's house.

You stole my many treasures and the blame and guilt is yours!
Someday you will answer to God for your many thefts.
Someday justice will be based on the evilness of your actions.
Today I leave the responsibility at your feet, where it belongs.
Today I was given a profound gift and hope for tomorrow.
I was helped to see your behavior in the truest light.
I choose not to be forever damaged by your multiple thefts.
I choose to fight to regain my stolen gifts, as that is my right.

I will grieve those stolen gifts that will always be blemished.
I will strive to be wiser and not cynical because of your thefts,
I will go forward strengthened in faith as I know the truth—
So many of my precious treasures were stolen, not lost!

Inspired by the Rev. Marie Fortune at the June 23, 1995, Kirkridge Retreat for Clergy Abuse Survivors.

CHAPTER THREE

Pastor Cool's Private Lessons

KATY

Pastor Cool thought he could cure me of my lesbianism. My encounter with him did result in a cure of sorts. Had he not abused me, I never would have addressed my issues the way I did, never would have had the opportunity to talk with other victims, and never would have had the money to escape the prison of the small town I lived in. Now I am able to set limits and to recognize when someone is trying to use me. And I no longer suffer from the low self-esteem that made me believe everything was my fault. Successful today in both my personal and my professional life, I know I can do anything I want to, because I have the will and I have control of my will like never before. Yes, the experience of confronting his abuse changed my life drastically.

Admitting my vulnerability is hard. I hate it when people react with sympathy. I want no sympathy. I am a survivor. But understanding the issues that made me vulnerable is essential to understanding *why* I was where I was *when* I was.

In the fall of 1989, I moved "home" to a place where, you might say, I'd never lived before. I moved from Florida back to Minnesota. My sole purpose was to start my life over again and to leave behind everything that had been me: drugs, alcohol, women, irresponsibility, selfishness, and all the deeply buried little secrets I intended never to share with a living soul.

My plan didn't work.

Oh, I got off to a good start. I went to church the first Sunday, eager to get back to the familiar liturgy, hymns, and people. I had known most of the people in the congregation for more than twenty years. Their faces hadn't changed. In fact, the only changes I noticed were that the shoulders were more stooped, the hair grayer.

Right away I was mesmerized by the newest addition to the church staff. The assistant pastor was younger than anyone else around, and I recall wondering how the elders had ever agreed to call a pastor half their age. Not only could this guy sing and speak, but I knew from having met him at my sister's wedding a few months earlier that he liked football and video games.

I felt as though I knew him well. My parents, who revered him and frequently invited him to family get-togethers, practically considered him a member of the family. There were several reasons for the close ties. Until I returned home, my parents had been empty nesters. My little sister, near the end of her college career, was now married. My brothers had long since flown the coop, and I had been away for ten years. Faith in God was as important to my parents as life itself, and it stood to reason that the comfort they found in Pastor Cool's company was due in part to that faith. He seemed to represent the holiness and goodness my parents had always found in the church. Furthermore, Pastor Cool's predecessor, a man who had led the congregation for many years, had been my father's counselor, spiritual guide, and best friend. When he was killed in a car accident in 1986, his absence left a void in my father's life. Pastor Cool filled that void.

I immediately recognized Pastor Cool as my savior, the answer to my prayers. I had been sinning for so long and had so much internal garbage to unload that I feared death and a literal hell.

I approached him after services that first Sunday home. He was kind and gentle, with clear blue eyes and soft, warm hands. His smile had friendliness written all over it. I told him about wanting to renew my membership. He suggested that we meet during the coming week to discuss my situation.

I was filled with the same sort of elation I associate with Easter, a renewed faith and realization that Christ is there for me, died for me, and rose for me. Before Pastor Cool even made it to our first session a sense of calm had already begun to come over me. I wasn't just going through the motions of affirming my faith this time; I truly felt the presence of God deep inside my soul.

My parents left for the East Coast a week after I got home. They gave me the responsibility of taking care of Grandma, who was eighty-nine. My mood changed. I was home alone, unemployed, and bored, and I didn't know a soul under sixty. I did the obligatory things for Grandma, like going to the bank for her, driving to the grocery, or running out for a jug of whiskey. I felt so sorry for myself that I decided to clean my parents' house from top to bottom. Anything was better than thinking. But the satisfaction that came with finishing the cleaning project quickly melted away, leaving me to deal with myself.

Within a day or two of my parents' leaving, Pastor Cool called to set up an appointment. He came to the house, which seemed perfectly normal, and brought a workbook with study guides. The book contained all the information I needed to renew my church membership.

I wasn't the least bit interested in the book. I remembered my confirmation classes as clearly as the day I'd taken them. But I didn't verbalize those thoughts, simply because I was unable to confront a member of the clergy on any issue. I had been raised to believe that men of the cloth were the next thing to Christ himself, and who on earth would tell Christ to take that workbook and put it where the sun don't shine?

What I wanted was spiritual guidance. I wanted to be forgiven of my sins, and I knew I had sinned more than just about anyone outside prison. I wanted someone to tell me it wasn't too late to save my soul from hell. I wanted far more than any stupid book could offer, more than I could get from praying alone. And I wanted it right away. Maybe I was looking for a shortcut, a quick fix, the easy cure. In any case, I wanted to get down to brass tacks, and that damn workbook was going to get in my way.

Nonetheless, after Pastor Cool's and my first appointment, I struggled through the first couple of chapters. I don't mind saying that my only goal was to have enough work done to get Pastor Cool back to the house and on about the business of saving my soul.

I was crazy with need.

The pattern of pastoral visits continued at about twice a week for the first few weeks. I obliged Pastor Cool by completing the work he asked me to do. We talked about my studies and little else.

I got a job working for a lawn service.

Fall had come to Minnesota, and I managed to take time to marvel at the changing of the seasons. I used my parents' car to take Grandma and my aunt for a ride to see the autumn colors. Years had passed since I'd considered the needs of others, but just being back in Minnesota made thoughtful gestures seem like the right thing to do.

Within a few weeks of my move home, I wrote a letter to an old girlfriend in Florida. She must have thought I'd lost my mind when she read my descriptions of watching the summer fade to fall, spending time with my aging grandmother, and going to church. The strangest thing had to be comments I made about wanting to find a man at church to marry. I wrote as though I was nearing menopause, talking about not getting any younger and needing to start a family before I was too old. I told her I was going to marry a Swedish farmer who could throw bales of hay.

I believed it all. The answer to all my problems was to change everything I was into something else, something socially acceptable, something that would fit the nature of the small Minnesota town I was again calling home.

Let's recap this briefly: an alcoholic lesbian moves home to Minnesota, swears off women, starts regular church attendance, and vows to marry a Swedish farmer.

While I was busy worrying about my transformation and trivial things like how to make my next car payment on four dollars an hour, Pastor Cool was in his office plotting. Though my parents had returned from their trip, my father's poor health made frequent visits to the doctor a necessity. Pastor Cool's close relationship with my parents made him privy to information most people cared little about, like when they were going to be at the doctor's office or on a daylong adventure. Inevitably, Pastor Cool would call while they were gone and rush over for our next appointment.

Then a bizarre thing happened. I came to the chapter in my workbook that dealt with confession and absolution. I wanted to skip that part. I did want to dump, to unload all the evil that polluted my mind, but "confession" sounded a bit too formal, and I wasn't sure I wanted the receptacle for my garbage to be a minister I liked. For twenty-seven years I'd managed to avoid confession and to keep my deepest, darkest secrets buried in the recesses of my mind.

All is still so fresh in my memory, the looks and sounds and smells of Confession and Absolution Day. It arrived like any of the rest of my Minnesota days, but it ended very differently. Pastor Cool explained that he would gladly hear my confession and that I should not fear pouring my heart out to him, for he was a messenger of God. Upon hearing my confession, he would grant me complete absolution, and I would be freed from the guilt that came with carrying such a heavy burden.

Tears welled from my eyes as I began to speak. I felt the presence of God deep inside and yearned to have the ugliness taken away and buried, buried anyplace but inside me, where it had eaten at me for years. Each year there had been a new sin to add to the list, and while I feared telling this man of God all the evil I had done, I feared carrying the load even more.

This was the chance I had been looking for, the reason I had moved back to Minnesota. I needed a fresh start, and no matter how much I moved, no matter where I went, nothing was going to change until I felt that release. My palms were sweaty and my voice shook. I hardly knew where to start. I felt older than dirt, trying to remember back to the first awful thing I'd done.

I would need a novel to cover my confession here, but making the move that day was as difficult as anything I've ever done. It was hard for me to tell bad things, really embarrassing events, to a minister. Worse yet, I had absolutely no self-esteem left. I thought that no matter what I said, Pastor Cool would think I was the lowest form of human life and would think my parents were scumbags for claiming me.

I think Pastor Cool was counting on that—all of it. He needed to see me at the humblest point in my life. He needed me to be afraid. Nobody before or since has seen me that low, that vulnerable. I poured my heart out. I told him everything I'd ever done: a list of people I'd slept with, many whose names I couldn't recall; the drugs I'd taken; and the things I'd done to get the drugs. I talked about my fear of AIDS, even though tests had repeatedly come back negative. I talked about having had sex with one of my brothers (though it would be two years before I understood I'd been the victim of incest). I talked about homosexuality and told how all my relationships with women had turned out badly, cost me money, and broken my heart. I went on for hours, powered by some invisible generator.

I cried. Pastor Cool smiled. I cried harder. He held my hand. It was touching really, so touching that it now turns my stomach.

Hours later, I was exhausted and wanted nothing more than sleep. I sure as hell didn't want to deal with any more things that could be added to the list of transgressions I'd just unloaded. But Pastor Cool wanted to console me. Actually, he wanted me to think he was consoling me, when really he just wanted an excuse to rub his hard little penis against me.

And that's exactly what he did. He wrapped his arms around me. At first, realizing that I'd started shivering, I welcomed the warmth. But instead of releasing me, he pulled me tighter and pressed himself against me. He pressed hard enough to make me aware that he had a hard-on and that the hard-on wanted to find its way to me.

I ignored it. Isn't that a good way to deal with things we are afraid to confront? Just pretend they aren't there, and they'll go away. Except it doesn't work that way. Pastor Cool left, but the feeling of his nasty boner pressing into my stomach stayed.

I faced a dilemma. I'd barely been able to wait to dump the embarrassing actions of my past onto someone. I believed that if I could just unload the burden, pour out my history of sins, the bad feelings about myself would go away. I needed Pastor Cool to like me, because he was going to save me from the evils of the previous life I'd just confessed. Yet I knew that guys like sex, and I knew that ministers of my denomination weren't celibate. Somewhere in life I'd learned that one way to make men like you is to have sex with them.

After Confession and Absolution Day I was reminded of Pastor Cool's parting embrace each time I saw him, each time I thought of him, and each time someone mentioned him. One morning the phone rang. It was too predictable. Mom and Dad had gone to Fargo or Grand Forks, North Dakota, for the day, and Pastor Cool wanted to come over. Having no notion of how to set limits and still wanting to complete my membership renewal, I consented. As I waited for him, the workbook I'd come to loathe seemed a welcome excuse to stay on task.

But we never got to it. Sitting in my parents' dining room, I found myself that day on the receiving end of confession. Pastor Cool poured out his disappointment over his marriage. (Until then I hadn't given any thought to the possibility that he was married.) His wife had married him, he claimed, for the security and visibility that came with being a minister's wife. She was involved in so many church activities that she spent more time at church than he did. And, he griped, she'd become fat and unattractive. As he kept up the barrage of words, he seemed to grow sad, tears welling from his eyes. He claimed to be stuck in his marriage, and his profession allowed no way out. After all, he was no layperson who could simply divorce the "bitch" and move on to another woman.

At first I didn't know who was talking. Only days earlier, this master of smooth talkers had impressed me with his caring, gentle nature, and now he was blasting his wife. Then I began to pity him. He was telling me a story much like my own, one of being trapped by personal history and finding the cycle repeated over and over until something drastic had to be done to change it. I'd made my radical move; he couldn't make his.

In my own pathetic way of believing what I heard, I began to take on some responsibility for his sadness. I cared deeply for this man—or at least I cared for the message of forgiveness he brought. I hope it makes sense when I say that I had to become his caretaker in order for him to remain mine.

It was time for Pastor Cool to go. He said he didn't want to be there when my parents came home. He spoke of not wanting the neighbors, most of whom went to his church, to think he spent an inordinate amount of time at my house. He sounded paranoid.

This time he made an issue of pressing his hard penis against me, letting me know it was there but not acknowledging anything verbally. He moaned lightly, the same way any of us might when we get a good hug. Then he bent down and kissed me, not even giving me the chance to refuse the tongue he slipped into my mouth. It was one of those experiences that is both scary and boring—he did nothing for me sexually. I just backed away, slipping from his embrace as I said goodbye.

I'm seldom at a loss for words, but the events of that day left me speechless. Though my heart reached out to Pastor Cool, I found myself wishing I still believed he was just a man of the cloth, just a minister there to save me from my own evils, a man whose own life was a model of Christian living.

It was one of those days when a drink was in order. And another.

The most startling realization came over me in waves: I was completely defenseless against his actions. Who do you tell that you've been kissing the pastor while your parents are away? I was racked with guilt and a host of other emotions, ranging from fear to panic. There was no way that God would absolve me from this sin.

The cure waited for me at the bowling alley, coming in the form of liquid served cold in a frosty mug. I consumed large quantities of beer and found that the more I consumed, the worse I bowled, but the easier it became to fill my mind with other thoughts. The wonderful result of my drinking was waking up the next morning unable to recall what was upsetting me so.

Not long after the kissing episode, I began to find notes on my car. Most were Hallmark cards, signed with a C. The cards professed Pastor Cool's love for me and his need for my body, and always included an urgent "I need to see you soon."

I still had a couple lessons left . . .

I hadn't done the Sunday membership ritual yet . . .

I needed this guy, but . . .

We never made it back to the lesson book. I'd been in Minnesota for about two months by this time, already resigning myself to the apparent fact that my life had not changed for the better at all. If anything, it had become worse. I'd gone from sleeping with irreverent, nonreligious women to trying to calculate how not to sleep with a married minister. Pastor Cool, however, found his way over to my house again.

I never figured out exactly what happened that day. It became one more situation I couldn't say no to, one more string of events that happened because I owned the patent on the fear of rejection. Our inevitable sexual rendezvous proved to me that I was forever incapable of doing the right thing. I knew it was wrong. I didn't want to. *I could not stop it from happening.*

So it did. Pastor Cool's visit started with Black Velvet and my mother's cigarettes and ended in the guest bedroom. For just one day, Pastor Cool told me, he could have the freedom to love the person he wanted to love, the one he would spend eternity with if he weren't trapped in his stinking marriage. His eyes filled with tears (give the guy an Oscar) as he held me close and told me I would never understand how his decision to enter the ministry had taken away his personal freedom yet how his bond with God was so intense he could never leave.

I believed everything.

During later visits Pastor Cool would tell me that the way we "did things" was the natural way, the way God meant sex to be. Everything about being with women was unnatural, and even though he couldn't leave his wife for me, he would give me the gift of knowing that sex with men was satisfying and that I would never need to seek women again.

Going to bed with him, though, was not at all what I wanted. So I started to avoid him. It was well into November, and I had a new job at a group home for delinquent youth. I attended church regularly, reinstated my membership, and started teaching Sunday school. I felt safer at church with so many people around, and God seemed to be with me there. I also felt sad at having betrayed God and often wondered if people knew I'd done something terrible. Even sober, I was paranoid.

Pastor Cool continued his visits, though they became less frequent. Three factors probably explain why he quit coming around so often. First, seven other church members were my parents' neighbors on "Church Row." Pastor Cool had run out of plausible reasons for coming over when my parents were gone. Second, there were indications he was working on at least one other victim. Finally, I gave as an excuse the world's longest-lasting menstrual period. It almost worked, except for the one evening when his tears persuaded me. To a certain extent I was flattered by his attention, which appeared more sincere than any I'd received before. The cards continued, sometimes accompanied by a tape on which he sang songs for me.

And could Pastor Cool sing! He could sing Bryan Adams as well as "The Lord's Prayer." He did "Mack the Knife" with the skill of a polished performer, and "My Way" as though he'd missed his real calling.

I stashed all his mementos in a safe place.

I kept my old job delivering pizza for a few months after I began working at the group home. Being busy distracted me. It also gave me excuses for turning down Pastor Cool's repeated invitations to his house. He was so brazen that he'd invite me to have dinner with his family or to watch a Sunday afternoon football game. I felt as if I lived in the twilight zone.

Pastor Cool wasn't one to give up easily, though. Sometimes he followed me on deliveries, stopping to chat after I dropped off a pizza. He'd tell me the lies he'd told his wife to get out of the house. As if nobody would see him in a town of six thousand. After a few months, he evidently got tired of chasing me. About six months after I'd moved to Minnesota, my only contact with him was at church.

I've heard that many people who work in social services or mental health arenas do so because they themselves need to be fixed. That must have been true for me. I could identify all my "issues" but never imagined that one might be connected to another, that using narcotics and alcohol had anything to do with my feelings of guilt or shame.

One day that all changed. A thirteen-year-old female client confided in me that she had been sexually abused by her twin brother. She told me her story through tears and said she was so embarrassed to admit that she had "let it happen." Never mind that he was much bigger; never mind that he threatened her with a steak knife—she believed she should have been able to stop him. Her story changed my life. I ended up in counseling for the next two and a half years.

During my first year of counseling, I quit drinking and started attending Alcoholics Anonymous. My counselor taught me that I couldn't resolve my issues by going around them, so when I came to the issue of incest, I plowed through it. I came to understand that my sexual relationship with my brother had been his sin, not mine. I was angry at him and found myself angry at my parents as well.

Sober, I was able to think clearly for the first time in years. I wrote my brother a letter, confronting him for what he had done and explaining the impact his abuse had had on my life. His first response was an angry accusation that laid all the blame on me. He also had the support of the family, so I alienated myself from them all for a while. Refusing to be whipped into their way of thinking, I spent Christmas away from my family for the first time in my life. They wanted me to forget about the abuse. After all, it had occurred many years earlier, and what had happened had happened. "You can't do a thing to change it now, so why make everyone suffer?" "Why wait so long to bring it up?" "You should have done something about it then." "Get over it; you're almost thirty years old."

I was furious. I convinced myself that my parents didn't want me to deal with it because they would have to share part of the guilt. They had known about the sexual abuse when it happened. What had they done about it? Dad beat my brother and Mom beat me.

I moved to another town, telling my family I wanted to be closer to college. In addition to enrolling as a full-time student, I continued to work full-time at the group home and faithfully went to my weekly counseling appointments. My therapist and I dove into everything, but I still didn't have the courage to tell her about Pastor Cool.

IT SEEMED THAT EVERY TIME I turned on the television or picked up a paper, there was a story about a priest or minister who had sexually abused someone. As I concentrated on getting healthier,

I came to realize that Pastor Cool had abused me, using his familiar relationship with my family and his position in the church to exploit my vulnerabilities. I was mad at him and even madder that I lacked (or thought I did) the self-esteem and confidence to come forward and confront him. I couldn't bring myself to speak out, for fear he would expose my sexual orientation and my promiscuous past. Even though I was aware of my right to keep my name out of the press, I knew the speed at which word travels in a small community.

Then the newsletter came. It was the church newsletter announcing that a voters' meeting would be held to decide about staff pay raises. Pastor Cool was up for review, and by all appearances he was due for not only a raise but a huge benefit increase. That was the last straw.

I could not let a man who pretended to be holy end up with a pay raise when Lord only knew how many men and women he'd had his hands on. So I armed myself, bringing in reinforcements in the form of my new girlfriend and my sponsor from AA. I practiced the words I wanted to say, then called the senior pastor and told him I needed to talk to him before the voters' meeting. At my insistence, we met on my turf, in my parents' house—the house where the vile deeds had taken place. My parents were spending the winter in Texas.

Quite frankly, the only thing I recall from the meeting is Pastor R.'s telling me he had been afraid my call meant I would tell him something like that. Did his words mean he or others knew of similar behavior in the past? If I'd been angry before, his response left me even more furious. If people in the church expected this kind of behavior, why hadn't Pastor Cool been supervised? Convinced that I had been exploited by the church as well as by Pastor Cool, I was more determined than ever to force the matter and bring Pastor Cool's actions out in the open.

By the end of the day, those present at the voters' meeting had asked for Pastor Cool's resignation and had escorted him from the church premises. I heard that he wasn't allowed to go home, for fear he would use one of the hunting rifles in his collection to end his own life. He spent the next few weeks in a psychiatric ward on suicide watch.

My disclosure that day was merely the beginning. I would recount my story time and again for the denomination's district board and for the attorney who took my case. I would also tell my story to other survivors, and the more I told it, the better I understood that I had no reason to feel the guilt and shame that had plagued me for years.

Disclosure became the first in a series of incidents leading to what I consider a remarkable recovery from everything that ailed me. For the first time in my life, I was confronting my worst fear—admitting the vulnerabilities that led me to become a victim. I was giving others permission to look behind the tough exterior I frequently put up.

I didn't go back to church after the day I told my story to Pastor R. I feared being rejected and labeled in a town that afforded no room to hide. I didn't have to go to church to find out that my fears were justified. People who would usually have greeted me at the grocery now turned their carts down another aisle. Some acquaintances did speak to me, telling me I shouldn't blame that poor man for the trouble I'd brought on myself. Clearly, they condemned me for exposing their pastor as an abuser and for bringing disgrace on their church.

It didn't matter though, the harassment I took. It only made me more determined to seek justice. The county prosecutor refused to press criminal charges, but my lawyer and I were successful in naming Pastor Cool, the congregation, and the denominational district as defendants in a civil suit.

I decided to sue because I wanted someone to be held accountable. Once it dawned on me in counseling that I was seeking help for the very issues that had made me vulnerable to Pastor Cool's advances, I realized there were hundreds of others in the same situation. I believed, and still do, that accountability makes people and institutions rethink the situations and policies that allow abuse to happen.

As I brought suit, I had to draw on the strength that other people assumed I had. In truth I felt like Jell-O inside. My love for food vanished, and my weight dropped dramatically. I wasn't able to concentrate on anything else, and I feared what I thought was the inevitable blast from the press.

It never came. The church wanted the whole business kept quiet, of course. The local newspaper caught wind of the story and questioned Pastor R., but he'd received word from his superiors not to talk.

Few people had the courage to support me. Perhaps my greatest disappointment was that even those at the nonprofit, church-affiliated organization I worked for discouraged me from taking legal action. They contended that Pastor Cool had already been removed from his capacity as a minister, so why drag it out? What was the point? The message I got was, "Abuse is bad, but look the other way if someone we know is the abuser." The administrators at the group home weren't brave enough to fire me; they simply made me feel so uncomfortable that I quit. I was now without a job.

I think the church hurried to rid itself of Pastor Cool to avoid accountability for its own failures. I learned that prior to my abuse, the church had not conducted a background check on any of its clergy or staff. Clergy were completely unsupervised and free to make up their own rules as they went along. The denomination had not instituted an abuse awareness program, nor was there a hot line like some other churches have. It was as if Pastor Cool were simply a problem child. By taking away his authority, the church believed it had remedied the situation. Local and district leaders were unwilling to investigate who else might have been harmed by his behavior.

Their approach didn't work. Another victim came forward shortly after I filed suit. During the attempt to pursue a criminal investigation, yet another one turned up. How many more were there?

Waiting was the hardest thing I had to do. I wanted to leave town but lacked the funds to go anywhere. I'd been forced to take a job making considerably less money. Meanwhile, Pastor Cool had moved to the small town where I was going to college. I quit school. I couldn't stand the thought of a confrontation with him outside a supervised environment. Every time I saw a car like his, I found myself looking over my shoulder. Paranoia was wrecking me.

When my parents returned from wintering in Texas, I knew I had to tell them what was going on before someone else did. I had been keeping them informed about the case at church but had omitted naming myself as the one abused. They'd hardly entered the door before I had them seated at the dining room table. Even now I remember thinking how weird it was to be sitting where I'd sat so many times with Pastor Cool. Now, my parents across from me, I was shaking like a leaf and felt as if I would lose control of all my bodily functions.

I started by telling them that I was the victim who had brought suit against the church. I finished by telling them there was something else they had to know: "I'm a lesbian. I moved in with a woman. It's someone you know. By the way, I love you both very much and I am very scared, nervous, upset, anxious, distraught, sick to my stomach, and I know you will stand by me because you've always taught me to stand up for what I believe is right . . ." I was talking a mile a minute. Though I'd anticipated anger and disgust, they handled my news remarkably well. A few nights later, my father invited my partner over for dinner while I was at work. He genuinely liked her.

Nearly a year after I'd first spoken with Pastor R., I received word from my attorney that the settlement hearing would be held. My attorney cautioned me that even though the church wanted to settle, it would push for a small amount by claiming I was damaged goods.

He was right. The church's attorneys argued that because I had a history of "sexual deviancy," drug and alcohol abuse, and strained relationships with family members, I was already damaged. I claimed that those very issues had made me vulnerable and that since Pastor Cool knew I had already been victimized, I was easy prey for him. I'm still furious over the arguments that day.

We reached an agreement in a matter of hours. Enough damages were awarded to pull me out of debt and allow me to relocate. Having had my personal life exposed in such a small community, I needed the opportunity to start over.

My settlement check came on February 4, 1994. I'd already given notice at my job and was preparing to move, but my partner and I thought a quick trip to Texas, where my parents were spending the winter, would be a good idea. Being far from Minnesota would offer a chance to unwind without having to look over my shoulder.

But first, I thought it would be fun to surprise my parents by depositing some cash in their checking account. It was money I'd owed them for many years. Dad called on the night I made the deposit to tell me I'd just about given my mother a heart attack. When she'd gone to the automatic teller to withdraw money, she'd seen the balance in the account and was shocked. Dad pressured me to tell how much I'd received, but I refused, explaining that confidentiality was part of the settlement agreement. We agreed to talk again on Tuesday night.

At 2:00 P.M. on Tuesday, my mother called.

"To what do I owe the honor?" I asked.

"Your dad died this morning."

As I burst into tears, my first thought was that I regretted not telling him about the settlement. That's how heavily the situation weighed on my mind. Even with the news of my father's death, I was thinking about the lawsuit and all I'd been through.

As relatives arrived from around the country and the house filled with guests, I began to realize that Dad's funeral would be at the church. I made a commitment to myself and to my mother: I was going to be a pillar of strength for both of us, regardless of how I was received by congregational mourners. And I did just that. I held my head high and ignored the many who chose to pass by me without speaking. I kept my arm around Mom, consoling her in a way that also comforted me.

Don't misunderstand. I felt eyes burning into the back of my head, and I knew I was the topic of more than one conversation. I just didn't care. That Valentine's Day, as I attended my father's funeral, I learned that I had moved forward and was happy to leave behind those who were stuck in their critical ruts.

MY LIFE IS DRAMATICALLY different now. My partner and I have weathered some difficulties in the adjustment to our new life. Probably our hardest time was caring for my mother during the nine months prior to her death. Two years after my father died, she was diagnosed with cancer. We kept her at our home, providing all of her care except for some assistance from hospice. During her last four days, we stayed with her around the clock. We both held her hand as she died. Though my mother and I were never best friends, I miss her and wouldn't exchange the experience of being with her for anything.

My partner and I make occasional trips back to the town of shallow minds, but only to see those few friends still living there. We live in a medium-sized metropolitan community, big enough for us to blend in whenever we want to. No longer do I have fairy-tale dreams of what I might and might not do, who or what I might marry, or what I'll be when I grow up.

We have a Gay Pride flag hanging from our porch.

I am not a vulnerable adult anymore. I stayed in counseling up to the conclusion of my civil suit, learning plenty about myself and others. I learned to set limits, though I still have a hard time saying no at work.

At one point I wondered how God could have let something like Pastor Cool's abuse happen to me. Now I believe it was a test of my will. Obviously I have the will to survive. Believe me when I say I have survived in the grandest style.

My biggest struggle is getting to church. I don't doubt my faith or the existence of God, and I accept Jesus as my savior. What I cannot accept is an organized religion that judges people who are different from the status quo and blames victims. Maybe someday I will find the church that fits me, one where I can share my story and be respected for the courage to stand up for what I believe.

For about thirty-three years I merely endured life. I took what came and lacked the ability to change it. Fear of rejection gripped me; I was strong on the outside and pathetically weak on the inside. The strength I gained through my experience cannot be measured, but I need only look at the life I enjoy now to quantify the change.

I've washed away all fears of being rejected. In fact, I am now a licensed realtor and face rejection all the time. I approach people with confidence, openness, and honesty. I have nothing to hide, because I have dealt with practically everything.

Clergy abuse, and my case in particular, used to be at the forefront of my mind all the time. It controlled me; it consumed me. I looked for every opportunity to tell someone about it, then was scared when I did. Maybe it's that struggle with my fears that led to my becoming so successful. The fascination of my abuse has worn off, thankfully, though there was a time when I thought I'd never think of anything else.

There is life after abuse, but I found it by going through it instead of around it, just as my counselor advised me. I had to face it and live with the ugly implications: being blamed, shamed, taunted, and teased. If I can find healing, most people can.

Though I'm not consumed by my experience anymore, I continue to tell my story. The more people who know about clergy abuse, the less likely it is to be repeated. People need to understand that abuse isn't something that happens only to children; it can happen to anyone who is vulnerable. And abuse isn't something people let happen. It definitely isn't the victim's fault when it occurs.

I'M HAVING FUN NOW. Since I've come back to reality, I've enjoyed a long-lasting relationship with my partner, who is Swedish but isn't male and probably can't throw a bale of hay any better than I can.

My work gives me tremendous pleasure. I make people laugh, and clients are comfortable with me. I don't pass judgment on anyone; I know what it's like to be on the receiving end. Though I don't trust everyone, I at least try to give people a chance and usually end up with clients nobody else wants. At least they want me. We get along great.

While I will always miss my mother and father, away from their watchful eyes I feel freedom like I've never felt it before. Still, their faith is a constant source of comfort. They kept it through their own ordeals and then, in their later years, through mine.

If their faith can survive, mine can too. Sometimes God allows the strangest things to happen in order to test our faith. I passed the test.

CHAPTER FOUR

And the Truth Will Make You Free

HOPE

I was tired of patting myself on the back because I hadn't committed suicide. I was tired of protecting my abusers and feeling all the guilt and shame. I wanted to give my children more, and I wanted to protect them from being victimized someday. I decided to deal with the issue head-on. Being a survivor wasn't enough for me anymore. I wanted to thrive.

THE VICTIM'S STORY

Life was good in 1974. I was a high school sophomore in a small Midwestern town with a population of three thousand. Everyone in town knew everyone else. I was dating Ken, a junior in high school, and was involved in the athletic and academic activities that a normal high school girl would participate in. I ran track and played basketball, volleyball, and softball.

I was the middle child of three girls and lived with both my parents. We attended church every Sunday and tried to do what was right, as defined by our Anabaptist heritage. I believed what I heard from the pulpit and looked up to my pastor with trust and respect, believing he had been called to be our shepherd and to lead us to righteousness.

During my sophomore year, our church hired a young associate pastor. Jacob Lansing brought with him the much-needed spark of enthusiasm and laughter that would help ignite our dying congregation. One of my first contacts with him occurred on a youth retreat soon after his arrival in town. As we gathered around the campfire, I shared with Jacob and the kids in my small group how happy I was to have him and his family in our church.

People respected and admired Jacob, so I felt fortunate when he began paying attention to me. We shared many personal conversations in his office, where the door was always kept open. I was a typical teenager who needed a trusted adult to talk with—about problems with boys or girlfriends or about how my parents didn't understand me. There wasn't anything I couldn't say to Jacob. In my young mind he was more than a pastor; he was my mentor, father figure, and best friend.

During my senior year in high school, I learned that the church secretary was leaving for a summer mission assignment in India. Great, I thought, I could have a summer job to make some money for college. Ken and my parents approved of my applying, especially because Jacob's and my relationship was so close.

My job interview was to take place after school and before track practice. Team pictures were going to be taken that day, so I knew I needed to make it back to school as soon as possible. After I arrived at Jacob's office, we made small talk for a time, then walked across the hall to the secretary's office, where he wanted to show me how to make appointments. He took a seat behind the desk. Before saying anything, he pulled me down on his lap and proceeded to explain the procedure. I couldn't figure out what was happening and was too paralyzed to challenge him or even to ask questions. We then walked back to his office, and for the first time in the two years we'd talked there, he shut the door. He sat beside me on the love seat.

A few months earlier, Ken had given me a promise ring, which I was very proud of. Jacob removed it from my finger. "Why would you want to get married?" he asked. He then spoke of how unhappy he was in his marriage and how difficult his wife was to get along with. He began playing with my hair, continuing to talk about the absurdity of marriage. "If I were to ask you to kiss me at work, would you?" he asked all of a sudden. I remember two of my thoughts: one, my parents had always told me that if there was one person you could trust, it was your pastor; and two, if I said no, maybe I wouldn't get the job.

I had always been a people-pleasing person who couldn't stand anyone's being angry at me. Not only did I want to please Jacob, I also wanted my parents to be proud of the initiative I had taken in getting a job. So when I was about to leave and Jacob asked, "Do you want to end this meeting with a kiss?" I could only shrug my shoulders. I was too numb, confused, and disappointed to say no. The confusion was due partly to knowing it was wrong to kiss somebody else's husband and partly to my sense of betraying Ken. Jacob assured me it was okay because I was special to him, and we would keep the kiss a secret. My best friend, my father figure, my pastor, was pressuring me to make decisions totally inappropriate for a teenage girl.

The interview did end with a kiss—a rather serious, involved one. I left for track practice late, of course, and missed the team picture. I still clearly remember how I felt that afternoon running around the track, seeing my teammates but not connecting with them. I felt different than I had felt three hours earlier. I smelled the green grass and saw the blue spring sky, but I couldn't relate to it anymore. Life as I understood it had vanished into thin air.

That day Jacob stole something from the sacred heart of a young, inexperienced teenager. My spirit separated from my body. My mental growth ceased. I remained like an eighteen-year-old for many years.

When Ken came over that night, he immediately knew something was wrong. When he kept asking, "What's wrong?" I finally broke down and told him. He vowed to confront Jacob the following morning, which frightened me. I had told Jacob's and my secret.

Jacob promised Ken he would never touch me again and begged Ken not to tell anyone. Ken left the office believing Jacob. The problem with this meeting is that no one was processing the betrayal with me. Two men were discussing a problem that involved me without my being there to speak for myself. How could they know how deeply the incident had affected me? How could my healing occur under these circumstances?

I did not get the job. For the next three and a half years, Jacob and I continued meeting in his office for counseling and conversation. He didn't keep his promise to Ken, though, and now closed the office door every time we met. My sexual curiosity was at its height. Having sexual experience, he knew how to touch me, knew how to turn something forbidden into something exciting. Touching and kissing evolved into heavy petting, which included his penetrating my vagina with his finger. Even though Jacob begged me to have intercourse with him, I refused because of my fear of getting pregnant. Looking back now, I see that my ability to say no was a sign of some strength.

I still attended church with Jacob as my pastor. One day he would beg me to go to bed with him, and the next day he would perform a marriage ceremony for two of my high school friends, eloquently speaking about marriage vows and how important commitments to our spouses were. People hung on every word of his sermons. They adored him and thought he could do no wrong. I would sit Sunday after Sunday, wedding after wedding, knowing the real man. Sometimes I pictured myself standing up in the middle of his wonderful sermon and telling him to fill in the blanks, to tell the truth.

As a teenager I had an idealistic view of the world. I looked forward to having freedom and power to make decisions on my own. When Jacob crossed the boundaries, he stole the freedom and power I was striving for. The only power he left me lay in the secret and in the fact that if I told anyone, he would lose his job and family. What a heavy responsibility for a young person who is just beginning the search for herself.

I remained confused over why I liked his attention. He made me feel special yet he made me feel like a whore. My thinking went something like this: Jacob is married, and I have a boyfriend. Jacob is good, but what happens between us is bad. Therefore, I must be bad. And the fact that I like the sexual excitement shows what a bad person I am.

Two years after graduation from high school, Ken and I got married. I knew it was a mistake; I was still lying to him about my relationship with Jacob. During the wedding ceremony, when I was saying my memorized vows to Ken, I skipped over the part where I promised to forsake all others. The memory lapse left me shaken. I guess God was trying to tell me something.

Marriage was a struggle and a very lonely time. It was hard for me to get close to Ken, because I felt like a cheat. Though I had assured him that my relationship with Jacob was over, I still visited Jacob in his office, and our encounters were sexual.

When Ken found a letter from Jacob asking me to run away with him, all hell broke loose. We were young and didn't get proper counseling. Ken loved me so much, and he had a right to want my relationship with Jacob to stop.

Meanwhile, Jacob's secretary became concerned about my frequent visits to the church and the comments Jacob made to her about our relationship. She met with the chairperson of the elders, who confronted Jacob and insisted that he end our relationship immediately. Soon afterward, Jacob left a letter in my car, telling me there were to be no more phone calls or visits. He had a family, a wife, and church commitments, he wrote, and he wanted to be faithful to them. I felt like trash that had been thrown to the wind. Jacob was the one who had dragged me into this hell, and only now he was deciding that his family and church obligations were important. Why hadn't they been important in the previous two or three years? I had become so emotionally attached to him that it seemed impossible to survive without him.

Who could help me? Ken, my parents, and a few of my close friends knew what had happened three years earlier at the job interview, but only God knew the whole story. And God didn't seem to care. In a community where Jacob was so highly regarded, no one would understand the web in which he had entrapped me. No one would believe what had happened in the pastor's office.

The request that Jacob not see me seemed a repeat of Ken's confrontation of Jacob several years earlier. The church cared about Jacob's and its own image, while I was unimportant, invisible. Why hadn't anyone talked to me? Where was the church that preached love and concern for a person's pain? Yet if the church were to express concern for me and if I were honest, would anyone believe me or care enough to do anything? Or would they feel sorry for Jacob?

I did not talk about our relationship until twenty-one years later.

Ken and I moved to a university town three hours away so he could attend law school. For most of our three years there, he was busy with his studies, leaving me lonely and depressed. I enrolled in college but couldn't concentrate. My mind was always on Jacob. I couldn't finish assignments and didn't care about anything. Life was such a struggle that on many days I welcomed the thought of death. Looking back, I feel cheated of my carefree younger years. I was dealing with serious dysfunctional adult problems but getting no help.

During the summers, Ken and I moved back to our home community to work at jobs in a large town nearby. One summer I confided to a high school friend that I needed to talk to someone who could help me with my struggles with depression and the desperate fear of losing my mind. She gave me the name of her former pastor, Daniel Miller. I had known Daniel all of my life.

When I was a small girl, he'd been a college student and had gone on to become pastor of a neighboring church in our denomination. Daniel, like Jacob, was highly respected in town. Good-looking, silver-tongued, and charming, he was viewed by the church as a wonderful, caring shepherd.

I called Daniel to set up an appointment. When I arrived at his house, he suggested we take a drive so we'd have more privacy. He drove me out of town about eight miles, to a deserted park. I had no choice but to trust him; I needed help in overcoming the agony with which I had been living for such a long time. I told Daniel about Jacob's abuse, giving all the gory details to this "man of God." By sharing my innermost fears and sorrows, in a way I was entrusting my life to him.

These were the first words out of Daniel's mouth: "Well, you will not believe this, but I have been attracted to you since you were a freshman in high school."

"Oh shit, here we go again," I blurted. I had entered the counseling session feeling dirty and sluttish. Sitting there in his car, I felt even more shame come flooding over me. A man wanted sex from me, and I was again in a situation where I had no control. I could only think, what have I said or done to ask for this experience again? Where the heck is God? At the park that day, Daniel kissed and touched me intimately. I had gone to him to help me deal with Jacob's having crossed boundaries, and now he was crossing them too.

I remember getting little sleep that night. I had learned so well how to conceal my feelings that Ken didn't know anything was going on. I was an expert at deceiving. It was my only way to survive.

Over the next three years, Daniel would tell me I was his special flower. I was his bud that he had put in his treasure chest, and now it was time for me to come out and become a beautiful blossom. Thinking about his metaphor today, I know that before he and Jacob got their hold on me, I *was* a blossom, so fresh and new. They turned me into a dandelion, but today I'm proud to be one, firmly rooted, persistent. No matter how often people try to chop me off, I just keep coming back. Sometimes I wonder why we dandelions aren't valued more.

Again I was under a minister's spell. The consequence of being controlled by someone else is that you have no goals or inner direction. Secrecy and an unethical man consumed the energy I needed for maturity. My growth was stunted. From my experience I understand how Jim Jones's followers could have been mesmerized. Once again, the only positive strokes I received were from an abuser who told me I was special and that this would be our secret. I was so dependent on Daniel, so anxious to please him, that I could think of little else. To feel okay about myself, I needed to communicate with him and be touched. I felt dirty but also special. I believed I was the chosen one, when in fact I was fulfilling another man's selfish needs.

As our relationship became fully sexual, my life became more and more out of control. I found it harder to maintain a relationship with Ken. The pressure was so enormous that I again thought death would be a welcome relief. I was involved not only with Daniel but with other men as well. Their attention gave me a high, like being on drugs. While the attention of other men propped up my self-esteem, taking my mind off the reality of what was happening and protecting me from being alone with my thoughts, I was in fact losing my dignity and what little sense of self-worth I had left. I became the expert at deception. I could have written a manual giving examples and methods of lying and cheating on your husband. I was so busy keeping my lies in line that it became a full-time job. Yet I felt guilty that Ken didn't know the half of what was going on. Available and vulnerable to other perpetrators, I wasn't safe anywhere, simply because I could not protect myself by saying no. It was as if I wore a neon sign on my forehead that said Screw Me.

It will always be a mystery to me what my marriage to Ken might have been like had I not suffered these traumas. After seven years of marriage, I couldn't take the constant worry that he would find out about my relationships with other men. The weight of the secret was burying me alive. I knew no way to survive but to leave him.

Daniel had often spoken of leaving his wife and marrying me. My divorce increased his desire. I convinced him to stay with his family, making the case that he would miss out on his three boys' getting married and having families of their own. I couldn't see how marrying him would solve any of my problems.

When I started dating my current husband in 1984, one of the first conversations we had was the truth about my relationships with Jacob and Daniel. Not sure what people in town thought or knew, I didn't want to take any chances that stories would get back to him.

But I didn't tell anyone else. I remained loyal to my perpetrators for many years. I had been their chosen one and didn't want to disappoint them. They were the people I had cared about most, the ones I had told my secrets to. Also, both Jacob and Daniel had convinced me that if I told, I would destroy their families and careers. That belief weighed heavily on me, because I didn't want anyone to hurt the way I was hurting. If I told the truth about these two men everyone admired and trusted, I wouldn't be believed anyway. After all, Jacob and Daniel had baptized people's children and buried their parents. One abuser, maybe. Two? I'd be seen as a seductress.

The Survivor's Story

It took me years to recognize and accept the truth that both Jacob and Daniel betrayed the trust I had placed in them and that what they did was wrong. They had never really cared for me as a person but had taken pleasure in having power over me.

All the while I just survived. I kept my head above water long enough to get a breath of air so I would be able to handle being underwater a bit longer. I lived with depression and low self-esteem.

I also became anorexic. That was one choice I could make—whether or not to eat. It was a way to make sure I was unattractive to men. It was a way to disappear from this messy world. Dying of starvation seemed much cleaner than a gunshot wound or a car wreck. I loved the empty, gnawing feeling that came with not eating. If someone mentioned I looked thinner, I'd be motivated to eat even less.

Again I was getting to a place where I wondered if life was worth continuing. Even though my husband and I lived far from my hometown and the relationships with Jacob and Daniel had ended, I carried the burden of shame and guilt. It was too heavy.

Fourteen years after Jacob's abuse had started, my husband and I, along with our two children, moved back to my hometown. We moved so that our children could attend good schools and be near their grandparents.

My family had to choose between the two churches that Jacob and Daniel had pastored. Jacob no longer lived in the area. After divorcing his wife, he'd moved and married his secretary (not the same one who had told the chairperson of the elders about Jacob and me). Daniel had left the ministry but still lived in town and attended the church he had previously pastored. Our family decided to attend that church, and we worshiped there for several years.

The past would come back to haunt me. I felt extreme guilt and believed I needed to protect Daniel, my new life, my marriage, and my family. It was as if a huge suitcase were permanently chained to my leg.

I coped by staying busy with other people's lives and problems. Raised in a Christian environment and taught to help others, I thought that if I solved other people's problems, mine would somehow disappear. I also continued the coping mechanism of starving myself.

Meanwhile, my family was suffering because of my dysfunction. During my children's most tender years, I struggled many mornings to get out of bed to change their diapers or feed them. They and my husband became secondary victims of Jacob and Daniel, and I fear my grandchildren will someday pay a price as well.

I attended church on a semiregular basis. God had betrayed me, I thought, by allowing not just one but two shepherds to abuse me. And since the pain hadn't been taken away, God must be enjoying my misery.

I also struggled with my Anabaptist heritage. Our stand for peace brainwashes us to believe that violence involves a gun, or blood and guts. If we don't see obvious damage on the outside, there must not have been any violence. The violence of sexual abuse is enormous but hard to measure, impossible to see with the eye. For me, the church's silence on the issue of clergy sexual abuse has been as violent as any physical injury could have been. For nearly twenty years I would have welcomed a gun to my back; now it will take a bullet to shut me up.

Later, when I brought accusations against the two men, I came to resent other parts of the tradition. The church expects a good Christian woman, if she's been victimized, to forgive and forget. Under the guise of living peacefully with all people, our heritage avoids confronting the hard issues. The code of silence doesn't allow healing for the victims or the perpetrators.

Life as a survivor became tedious. I was putting one foot in front of the other, hoping not to fall flat on my face. There were days that seemed to go on forever, and the pain was so intense that every bone in my body ached and I felt a constant gnawing at my heart. "Where is God?" I would ask. I hated myself and everyone else, especially happy people who seemed to have it all together. I read self-help books, such as *When Bad Things Happen to*

Good People, and *I'm OK, You're OK*. I tried several counselors; however, I couldn't trust anyone, man or woman.

THE THRIVER'S STORY

It wasn't until I attended "Hope for the Journey," a conference sponsored by local churches, survivors of sexual abuse, and a mental hospital, that I realized I could do more than survive. A year later I heard Miss America of 1958, Marilyn Van Derbur, tell her personal story of sexual abuse as a child. She spoke of truth telling and said that if we don't vent the poison inside us, we will deteriorate and become emotionally paralyzed. Over and over she repeated that we have to do that work. I realized then that to thrive would require hard work and that *I* would be responsible for doing it, not anyone else. I wanted to deal with my problems in a constructive way instead of being destructive to myself and continuing to let my abusers control me.

I asked myself, how am I going to do this? I still had a hard time believing that God willed me to be a happy, healthy person. Determined to give God another chance, I decided to take God's hand and let God lead the way. I was going to have to give up my attempts to gain control over my life.

Another step toward healing came when I made a phone call to Pastor Leland, pastor of the church Jacob had served. As soon as I told him the whole story, I could tell that he was different from my abusers, that he had lived a life of integrity and faithfulness to his wife. He understood my pain, and he was angry at the church and at my perpetrators for what had happened to me. He said the information I provided now helped him understand the congregation's dysfunction. Finally I'd found a pastor I could trust.

After deciding to thrive, I struggled for many months, impatient for God to show me what healing required. How would I heal? How would I feel? Would I really feel better, or would I maybe feel worse? If I felt better at first, when would the honeymoon end? I decided to sit and be silent. Spiritual friends prayed when I no longer thought it worth the effort. Without my friends I might not have made it.

Meanwhile, Jacob's ex-wife, Mary, and I became acquainted. She was trying to get her life back together after he had divorced her. She and I were seeing the same counselor, and independently we each expressed our wish to talk with the other. She wanted to hear my side of what had happened between Jacob and me; I was trying to make restitution with people I had hurt. Our counselor brought us together in a meeting that was, to say the least, difficult. Mary's first comment, when I finished telling the story, was, "If I called him and told him what you said, he would call you a liar."

Over time we were able to speak honestly and listen to each other's hurt. She described his abusive behavior toward her; I spoke of the damage he had done to my life. Our friendship has grown, and many in our small town are still shocked to see us in public together.

One Sunday, when I knew Pastor Leland was going to preach a sermon titled "Healing Our Painful Pasts," I decided to attend his church. His three points were very clear: First, name the pain, face it, bring it to the surface. Second, tell someone you trust. Third, give your pain to God. Moved by his words, I wondered how the three points applied to me. *Name it. Face it.* I decided not to protect Jacob and Daniel any longer. I had been caring for them more than for myself. I wasn't going to worry about their lives and about how disclosure would affect their families. I waited and listened some more for God's quiet voice.

Tell someone you trust. Give your pain to God. God told me to have a healing service where the abuse had begun twenty years earlier. So I invited sixty people who were significant to me in some way. I personally called them and told them what the service was for. To my surprise, all sixty were able to come that night. One guest who was especially important to me was Mary. She and I had already started to build our relationship, and I was moved by her willingness to come.

I shared with no one, including my husband, what was going to happen. I planned the complete service—the readings, songs, symbols—and wrote the story of the abuse. Keeping everything secret eliminated my having to defend what I wanted to do. For one time in my life, I cared more about what I needed than about people's approval. I felt confident and empowered.

That night was a turning point in my life. While I waited in a hallway off the sanctuary, Pastor Leland began the service with a short welcome and prayer. Then I entered the sanctuary through the side door, dressed completely in black—black dress, black hose, and black shoes. I had cut a letter A out of red tape and had attached it to my chest.

To my right and left stood two friends, also victims of sexual abuse. Around my neck, tied in strips of bedsheets, I wore thirty pounds of rocks, which caused me to stand bent over. As I started telling the full story in public for the first time, I began to cry. Oh great, I thought, I can't even get through the first line. Suddenly, though, I stopped crying and God started speaking for me. As I told the truth of the abuse, including the names of my abusers and what they had done, my two friends removed the rocks one at a time from around my neck and placed them on a table. Then, as I shared the feelings of guilt, shame, depression, hatred, and despair, the women beside me ripped the bedsheets. The ripping sound comforted me, because making my pain audible helped people understand how I had suffered. I was no longer alone.

When my story was finished, I took a hammer and crushed the limestone rocks as hard as I could. This showed how my spirit had been smashed. As I put the broken pieces into a bowl and cleansed them with clean water, I invited people from the audience to cleanse the rocks with me. In an emotional moment, Mary came forward to cleanse the rocks. Her standing beside me made a powerful statement about healing and reconciliation. Another moment of blessing came when I ripped the A from my dress and cast it to the ground, vowing never to wear the guilt and shame again.

The second half of the service took place at the church Daniel had pastored. Before leaving the first church, however, I changed into all-white clothing. As I removed the black dress, my body felt relieved of a tremendous weight. A good friend took the dress home. We would dispose of it later. People later told me that when I walked into the second church, I glowed.

At the first church I relinquished the pain of the past. The rituals at the second church were directed toward healing. In our tradition an anointing service is usually associated with physical healing. That night, however, it was for the recovery of my spirit. Placing a spot of oil on my forehead, Pastor Leland blessed me and prayed for my healing. I can only grope for words to express my emotions at that moment: overwhelmed with joy, free from the abusers' control, free from guilt and shame, understood. After a responsive reading, we sang the hymn "O Healing River."

Next we descended the stairs to the fellowship hall, where the group sat in a half circle. I had baked bread and set the communion table. One by one I served the guests, looking into their faces at their joy and sadness. Some cried. The service ended with our singing "God, Who Touches Earth."

A month later, at a significant crossroads in town, I met four friends and burned the black dress in the middle of the intersection. Such a billow of smoke rose that I feared the neighbors might call the police, even though I had cleared this activity with the chief of police and the fire chief. As I watched the smoke, though, I saw my past pain and misery being burned beyond recognition and felt a sense of control.

Personal confrontation with both perpetrators also contributed to my becoming a thriver. A year after the healing service, I met with Daniel Miller. For the first time, in front of others, I was able to share with him the lifelong effects his abuse caused:

the psychological damage and the divorce. What a selfish act it was, I told him, to take advantage of a young woman who was already wounded and who had come to him for help. Just as they had more than twenty years earlier, his eyes expressed sincerity. He said he was sorry and asked for my forgiveness.

Instead of saying the words he wanted to hear, though, I told him, "No, I won't forgive you. You need to take care of the other victims, and I don't think you have enough time on earth to do it." (I knew there had been others.)

Just because someone asks for forgiveness doesn't mean the person being asked is obliged to give it. Forgiveness can confuse us, leading us to forget what we need to remember. We can't help other victims by offering the abusers easy grace. I gave the guilt and shame back to Daniel, where they belong.

People who don't understand the damage of clergy sexual abuse sometimes urge us victims to forgive the abuser. He should be allowed back in the pulpit, they say. I use the analogy of losing your virginity. All it takes is one time. Once you've crossed the boundary, there's no way to get your virginity back. No matter how sorry you are about giving it up, your regrets don't do any good. Perpetrators can't undo what they've done. I say, if they still want to serve the church, let them fold bulletins.

I experienced some vindication when Daniel wrote a letter of confession and mailed it to 150 former members of his congregation and others. For me, the day the letters were received was a glorious one. What a miracle!

Six months later, I met Jacob Lansing, now a pastor in another denomination, for a confrontation at his former church. In front of him and nine other people, I once again read my story. The day before, I had blown out the insides of an egg and now had placed the eggshell in front of me. When I read about the brokenness and emptiness my spirit had suffered, I raised my hand, brought it down sharply, and smashed the eggshell with such force that I broke the skin on my hand. From the corner of my eye, I could see people jump in their chairs. I explained later that we could sit there for the next twenty years and try to put the eggshell back together, but it would never be the same. It would look different and would have permanent cracks.

I had made a red letter A for this occasion, too, and had tied it around my neck. When I shared with Jacob the guilt and shame I had been carrying around for him for twenty-one years and told him I wasn't going to carry it anymore, I took off the letter and threw it toward him. I told the group that the A was no longer mine to carry; Jacob would need to dispose of it.

At the end of my story, I turned off the lights in the room. We were in a basement with no windows, so it was dark. I let people sit in the room for a while so they could feel what it was like for me to have lived in the darkness of depression, isolation, and confusion. After allowing them to reach an uncomfortable stage, I lit a red candle. I asked the person on my right to light her candle and pass it to her neighbor. When the flame came back to me, I lit a white candle and blew out the red one. I shared that the color red reminds me of pain and blood, and white of cleansing and restoration. In the candlelight I read 1 John 1:5–10 from the Bible. Verse 8 says, "If we say that we have no sin, we deceive ourselves, and the truth is not in us."

I was facing my enemy. Jacob didn't respond. I think he was surprised to be confronted by someone he had once controlled but now had no power over. He acknowledged having kissed me but claimed I had made up the rest of the story. Seeing the way he reacted and his denial (to this day), I realized I was nothing to him.

He left the A on the table. I gave it to his supervisor and told him to destroy it. As I left the church that day, I felt strong and close to God. I don't think this sort of confrontation is for everyone, but I found it significant in my healing process.

I have never been sorry for insisting on all the experiences I needed to heal. I have been set free from the bondage of two trusted shepherds of God who themselves went astray. I can honestly say I now live as a thriver instead of just a survivor. I rejoice every day that God restored my life after twenty-one years of hell on earth. When I walked through the valley of the shadow of death, God was at the other end with arms wide open, saying, "Come to me; I will protect you."

I tried many methods to heal from the past—therapy groups, support groups, friends—but the biggest difference came when I told the truth to a group of people who had an investment in my story, either by knowing me or by knowing the perpetrators. Truth moved me from being a survivor to being a thriver. It rescued me from the poison that was killing me.

Telling the truth means telling the story without filtering the facts for fear we'll hurt someone's feelings. Sure, some people are offended; the truth requires that they help carry our burden. But why should we have to shoulder it alone?

"And you will know the truth, and the truth will make you free" (John 8:32). My prayer for all the victims of the world is that the healing power of God and truth may transform their lives.

CHAPTER FIVE

I Have Cried with the Psalmist

MIKKI

Yes, there is life after confronting an abuser and an abusive system. Yes, there is healing. Yes, there is opportunity to use one's gifts. Yes, there is opportunity to grow. But all these blessings that I embrace with gratitude do not make up for the losses. I am no less thankful, simply aware that I am not the same person I was. The abuse and my naming it have changed my life. The damage has been done, and I continually have to fight with myself not to be defined by the damage. I have had to come to terms with the fact that not all the holes in my heart will be filled.

Over and over I have replayed the events of Andy's abuse and the response of the Elder Board. I have agonized over what I could have done differently. I have questioned the whole situation: was it really that bad? After all, I wasn't raped; we did not have intercourse. The memory of actual events has become hazy over the years, yet I still have dreams about Andy—about being pursued, about bodies being dismembered, about being naked, exposed to the elements.

The process of writing my story, of my continuing efforts to understand and integrate my life, has been interesting. But I am afraid I will not be able to tell the story in a way that will lead the reader to understand the depth of fear, shame, terror, and betrayal I experienced. I am so afraid that you, Reader, will respond with, "So what's the big deal? Get a life. Lots of women have had worse things happen to them, and they don't call it clergy sexual abuse. You're just making excuses for your life."

To that I respond, you didn't live my life; you didn't live through the abandonment of childhood that shaped me, molded me in a way that made this betrayal of trust so devastating. I still don't have the confidence to tell myself, "So what if readers don't understand? I know what happened to me, and it hurt, and it was important, and nobody understood or cared."

DURING THE SUMMER OF 1977, prior to my graduation from college the following December, I went to a major city to serve as a youth worker at an urban church. My immediate supervisor was Andy, a seminarian who was completing his training in urban ministry. During the summer I became friends with him and his wife, Ellen.

In December I wrote to Andy and Ellen, wondering what I should do with my life after graduation. Andy responded with an invitation to join them in a new church-planting venture jointly sponsored by two denominations. The call to all of us participants in this fellowship was to come to live and work in the city; to be Christ's body and witness in a multiethnic, multicultural environment. It was a venture that would cross all sorts of boundaries—race, class, education, gender, language—and would confront all the "isms" that separate people from one another. It sounded like a wonderful opportunity to put my faith into practice. It appealed to my idealism, my desire to make the world a better place.

I arrived in late December and got a job as an assistant teacher at a neighborhood day care center. I lived with Andy and Ellen for a few weeks until I was situated in my own apartment.

Living on my own was a tremendous change. Even though I had left my parents' home at eighteen, I had never lived alone. Having been raised in a conservative, small-town church, I had been indoctrinated with its ideas of what constituted the Christian lifestyle: don't drink, smoke, swear, or even talk about sex. So I was ill equipped for the freedom and variety of lifestyles I found in the big city. I became friends with the other young women who were teachers at the day care center. We went to bars on Ladies' Night, drank and danced on the weekends, and looked for guys.

Occasionally a man would notice me. This was a new experience. As a teenager I had hardly dated, nor had I dated much in college. My family had always seen my weight as an issue, telling me I would never marry because I was too fat. So I was surprised when I began to receive attention from men—in particular, African American and Hispanic men, who, perhaps because of their cultures, didn't see being heavy as a liability.

I had no tools for dealing with men. The values I had grown up with—no sex outside marriage—were not always adequate guidance or protection. Besides, I felt a deep yearning for someone, some man, to love me. And though my head knew that sex does not equal love, my heart wanted to believe it did.

During those couple of years, I carried tremendous guilt about being sexually active. What if my mother found out? What if Andy or Ellen found out? What if others in the fellowship found out? Still, I kept believing that each new guy would turn out to be "the one."

Meanwhile, I remained a faithful member of the church-planting team. I knocked on doors, led Bible study groups, attended community meetings, and led worship services at a local nursing home. Frequently, Andy, Ellen, and I met together to strategize.

I also met separately with Andy for what he called "theological reflection." We talked about my life in the city and about what God was calling me to do. Andy had been trained specifically for urban ministry, and he was taking me under his wing. I had a pastor, a mentor, and in some ways a brother, for he took the place of my older brother, with whom I'd been close while growing up.

When Andy and I talked, I felt special. He raised my hopes that my talents could be used for God's purposes. He affirmed me as a woman. He challenged my beliefs about God, the church, and Christianity. He seemed to value my abilities and to see me not as an overweight woman but as a friend and a committed, talented church leader. The meetings also made me feel part of the team, part of the inner circle. My ideas were sought, even deemed important.

For at least thirteen years, Andy and I continued our meetings. Over time I shared nearly all the details of my emotional and private life. He knew about my painful family relationships. He knew that my birth father had been a batterer. He knew I felt ugly and unlovable because I was overweight. He knew I felt like a whore because of those years of promiscuity. He knew I worried about what others thought of me.

I trusted Andy. I idealized him. I wanted his approval.

Meanwhile, the church-planting venture gave Andy the opportunity to shape the church as he wanted it. We were building community, he said, and because of our idealism, the rest of us embraced the notion. We were so much one family that visitors to our services couldn't tell whose children belonged to whom; we all shared the responsibilities. And we freely expressed our affection with warm hugs.

Not everyone, however, valued being part of such a closely knit community. One woman who finally left the fellowship told me, "I get so sick of the C word [community]." Later, when I charged Andy with inappropriate behavior, people urged me not to dwell on my issues but to forget them. "For the sake of the community," I heard over and over.

Four years after joining the fellowship, I married Rich, who had come to the church as a seminary intern and stayed. I worked hard to be a wonderful wife—a Stepford wife (for those familiar with the horror movie about perfect wives). After only a few years, multiple stresses led me to begin sorting out my life with a clinical social worker.

A short time after my marriage, things began to change between Andy and me. During our conversations and reflections together, he began to make comments such as, "I have a physical reaction to your presence." When I talked about my marriage difficulties or my pain about my obesity and body image, he would respond with his desire to massage me, to heal me, to free me from my torment. I hated it when he made such remarks and always responded that I was not attracted to any men, even my husband, at that moment. This wasn't true, but I thought it would make him stop. The fact is that I was not then, never was, and never will be physically attracted to Andy. But, not wanting to hurt his feelings, I made it sound as if I had a problem with physical intimacy.

In our conversations Andy confessed that he also had problems with sexuality issues, that he often fought lust. Sometimes he spoke of how he would like to touch me and be close with me. He would laugh and joke that maybe one way to make money for the church would be for him to write erotic books.

It was a very confusing time for me. Andy was like an older brother whose approval I desperately wanted and needed. I liked spending time with him—getting his advice, hearing his take on situations, laughing at his quick wit. But being alone with him meant that I always had to worry that he would bring up his sexual desires—or even worse, that he would try to kiss me. These were not on-the-cheek kisses but the on-the-lips kind. To kiss him seemed too much like kissing my brother or father, so I always tried to turn my head and move away as quickly as possible.

Often I would try to steer him out into the worship room for our meetings, where people came in and out, but he always wanted to meet in his office. I remember that once, when I almost managed to leave without a kiss, he came up behind me, put his arms around my waist, and kind of nuzzled my neck. Anytime he tried to touch me, I stiffened, thinking that he would sense my discomfort, that my attempts at deflection would tell him this was not the kind of attention I wanted. But he never acknowledged my lack of response.

The tension for me was dreadful. I wanted the mentoring, but to have any relationship at all with Andy required that I pay a tremendous price. Our relationship was to be his way or no way, and after all the losses in my childhood, I feared losing him, too.

Meanwhile, our little church wasn't growing. Andy became increasingly cynical and began to fight bouts of depression, which grew worse when his father died. He took a year's leave to go to truck-driving school and work in cross-country trucking.

While he was gone, I began to carry out the major duties of the church, which finally led to my being licensed as associate pastor. In Andy's absence, two other elders and I began to meet as an administrative support team.

Andy's trucking career was cut short when, after about six months, Ellen gave him an ultimatum. She could not raise their three children alone, with him coming home only every other weekend, or even less often. He quit his trucking job and returned angry and disappointed.

He rejoined the administrative team, but now it was as if he were trying to unravel my new identity as a church leader. Without recognizing the leadership that any of us had provided in his absence, he took charge as if he'd never been away. Every idea, every action needed his blessing.

The most devastating incident between us occurred after a congregant's mother died. I had recently started seminary. Andy invited me to accompany him, for ministry experience, to a neighboring state to help with the funeral. I agreed to go. His son, Jimmy, who was ten or eleven years old, also went. On the way, the car began to malfunction and would go only about forty-five miles an hour. We finally got to the funeral home about ten minutes before the service was supposed to begin.

After the funeral we had dinner with the family. At about eleven o'clock that night, Andy was trying to decide whether, given the trouble with the car, we should drive back home or get a motel room and wait until morning. I was beside myself with panic.

What if he decided to stay? Would he try to get the three of us to share a room to save funds? Even if I had my own room, what if he tried to come over?

I was relieved when he decided to try to return home that night. As we traveled, with Jimmy asleep in the back of the station wagon, Andy began a conversation about sex, sexuality, and his physical attraction to me. We were on the highway in the middle of nowhere when he pulled off at an exit. I thought we were going to make a bathroom stop. Instead, he parked on the shoulder of the road, pulled me to him, and began to kiss me.

Frantically I considered my options. Here we were, in the middle of nowhere in the middle of the night. What if I refused and made him angry? Would he make me get out of the car and leave me there? Would he become violent? Even if he got back on the road and headed home, what would the rest of the ride be like? I decided to let him kiss me. Yet I kept wondering: What will happen if Jimmy wakes up? Will he tell Ellen that he saw his dad and me kissing?

I began to have what I call a "split." I hovered around the roof of the car watching another woman being kissed. It wasn't me; it was someone else. When Andy touched my breast, I pushed his hand away, saying, "No" and "I can't." Eventually he started the car and we drove on home. Along the way he told me he knew he couldn't live with me, but he would really like to have sex with me. For me the comment translated, "You're good enough to f— but not good enough to hang around for." His words confirmed my doubts, fears, and beliefs: I really was the whore I thought I was. Even Andy thought so.

Neither of us mentioned the incident later. I felt so much shame that I could hardly stand it. I should have pushed him away, I told myself.

Going back over my experiences with Andy, I now see details I didn't notice at the time. Just six months after he kissed me in the car, he again was my supervisor, this time for field education at seminary. In my mid-year evaluation, he identified vulnerability as the area I needed to grow in. He wrote, "[Mikki has] an inability to become vulnerable to others. Therefore she can feel quite unsafe around people who are different or going through crisis. . . . [Her] discomfort, insecurity and defensiveness in the midst of diversity makes it hard for others to be totally vulnerable to [her]." Those remarks were absurd.

Later, in the year-end evaluation, he wrote that in the last weeks of my field studies assignment, *I* had identified vulnerability as an issue to address. Just writing this now, many years later, makes me want to punch him, kick him, call him every vile name I can think of. *He* was the one concerned about my inability to be vulnerable with people. The irony is almost palpable. He was the one who had access to my stripped-down soul. He was privy to all my personal secrets, shames, disappointments, failures, hopes, and dreams. What he understood as my inability to be vulnerable was simply my meager attempts to protect myself from someone who already knew more about me than he would honor.

A student needs to know that a supervisor has the student's best interest in mind and that the supervisor will not intentionally harm the student. Instead of affirming me as he had done in the early years of our friendship, Andy now seemed to crave the opportunity to point out every shortcoming I had. No wonder I felt unsafe, uncomfortable, insecure, and defensive at having him for a supervisor. It was as if I had a target on my back toward which he constantly directed his criticism. Every task I performed was in some way inadequate, and he could show me how to do it better. His need for control took precedence. He was like a sponge, wanting more and more and more of my soul.

After a while, Andy's attention shifted to Cynthia, and the two of them began to lead the church in "undoing racism." Having known him for more than fifteen years, I recognized his pattern: embrace an issue, convince people to follow his lead, then lose interest and move on to something else. His sexual attention toward me stopped as he became more involved with his new project and began to sexualize his association with Cynthia. I felt outrage over their relationship. At the time I couldn't identify the reason. Now I know it was not because of jealousy but because for him, relationships were interchangeable.

Though I was now copastor of the church, Andy and I hardly spoke anymore. We did, however, have one conversation I remember well. He asked me, as one of the worship leaders, to begin planning worship from an African American perspective. By then I had gained confidence and felt I could challenge him. I expressed my concern that racism was not an issue that could be put away when he got tired or bored. I also challenged him about his relationship with Cynthia and asked if he would continue on this journey if she left. We talked and shared at a depth we hadn't had for a long time. Finally, because I wanted to please him and because of my support of our fellowship's antiracist agenda, I agreed to lead worship the way he wanted me to. Afterward, two things became clear: First, he'd manipulated me into doing worship his way by pretending we were still close. Second, I saw clearly for the first time that I'd lost my best friend.

A year later I began to understand better what had happened between Andy and me. As part of my job with a national agency of a mainline denomination, I attended a meeting that included training in dealing with sexual harassment and clergy misconduct. Having taken a seminary course on sexual and domestic violence and having talked with victims, I thought I was well versed on the topic. Suddenly, though, something clicked during this training, and memories about my relationship with Andy came rushing back. I began to tremble and had to fight back tears. I could hardly breathe. I wanted to scream. I was filled with a terror I couldn't explain. Here I was, far from home, with no one around to talk with.

After returning from the training, I called Andy. I called to discuss church business and to tell him how it was difficult to try to do church work without having any contact with him. He accused me of blocking the church's progress in working on racism and of having a very traditional view of ministry, one based on a social-work background. He didn't want to be part of a church that clung to the old racist way of doing things. He claimed to be having many problems with me, which I found difficult to understand, since we hadn't had a conversation for six months.

I told him I couldn't follow his leadership in undoing racism, because he had sexualized his relationship with Cynthia, just as he had with me. Because of this association with her, his leadership was compromised. I discussed our past relationship, describing how shamed I was by the kissing episode and how I felt dirty and embarrassed. I finally told him the truth: I had never found him attractive but hadn't wanted to hurt his feelings. The conversation ended with Andy suggesting that we meet for breakfast the following day to work on communication and collegiality. Like a dope, I agreed. My final words over the phone were, "I would leave the church before I harmed it." That's how much I loved the church and the people.

Over breakfast the next morning, he apologized for having read "the situation" wrong. I had trouble with our peer relationship, he claimed, and maybe there were times when I had come for pastoral counseling when he misread the situation. And he was sorry. All I remember about his reference to the car episode is that he said it just "sort of happened." According to Andy, it was my problem, because he had thought we had a peer relationship.

Not until a later conversation did I explain that we were not peers, had never been peers, and probably never would be peers. Our church structure, even when we had changed my title from associate to copastor, had never allowed for a peer relationship. His name was the only one on the church letterhead. He was the only one with business cards. He was getting more cash salary than I, plus social security and a housing allowance. He had an office; I did not. He could sign checks; I couldn't. It was not a peer relationship.

I had no intention of telling anyone of how Andy had sexualized our relationship. However, because I was so distraught after our breakfast conversation, I ended up telling my story to three church leaders. None of them expressed surprise. I even told my husband, leaving out some details. He wasn't surprised either. If no one was surprised, why hadn't anyone warned me years before?

At one point I told Cynthia I had to leave the church, that it was killing me. Because we were heavily into undoing racism, however, she asked me to put aside my personal problems to carry forward the work of the church.

I seriously tried to do that for several months, but the task became untenable. I would be fine until Andy walked into the room or until he spoke at a meeting or until he preached. If he was serving communion, I could not participate. Perhaps most painful of all, I didn't assist with communion, because I couldn't bring myself to extend the bread and cup to him. One of my most treasured privileges had been to serve communion to my friends and my family.

At times Andy would still try to pat me or touch my arm in a comforting, kindly gesture, and I would become frantic. I couldn't get out the words "Don't touch me!"

I stayed at the church because I believed the work of undoing racism was crucial and necessary. After more than a decade, our fellowship was still mostly white, but I believed in the dream of an interracial community. Today I see the irony of a church talking so much about racism but refusing to understand the abuse of women.

I also stayed because I was afraid of being alone. This was my family; these had been my closest friends for more than sixteen years. If I left, I would be without a community. But in many ways, I was already alone—and had been ever since I had begun to carry this secret.

The church was like an incestuous family. Daddy had taken advantage of one of the children, but the rest of the family didn't want to deal with it. Interpersonal relationships were so complicated and complex that it was difficult to separate personal issues from church issues. For me, the work around undoing racism complicated the matter even more. I was so afraid of what people would think about me. I feared that if I came forward, either I would not be believed or my experience with Andy would seem inconsequential compared to the church's work.

A year after I'd disclosed Andy's behavior to the three church leaders, a crisis erupted. Andy served as chair of the Elder Board, which was responsible for the spiritual leadership of the church. At a monthly meeting, I stated my desire to resign from the board. When board members pressed me for a reason, I told them Andy had acted inappropriately with me for several years, and I did not want to serve on the Elder Board with him. Interestingly, no one questioned Andy about whether or not my allegations were true, nor did Andy deny them.

That night the Elder Board accused me of using Andy's sexual misconduct as an excuse to get out of the antiracist work. Many of the values I held dear were used to attack me. One woman confronted me directly: "How can you let a man do this to you?" she asked. Later she said, "I have to know what to tell my children about you." Andy's behavior was never discussed. As they spoke, it was as if a wall went up around my heart and I was above the room observing this craziness. I left at that point, still physically present in the room but emotionally gone.

In essence, the Elder Board told me that if I chose not to serve on the board, I would need to make a complete separation from the church. So I sent a letter of resignation, effective immediately. Following my resignation, a representative from the board called to invite me to meet with them, but she called so late that I didn't have adequate time to find an advocate to accompany me. The church didn't want to lose me, she said. They loved me. They wanted to see healing between Andy and me.

I told her I wanted Andy to be held accountable. I suggested that he write a formal apology; that he resign as chair of the Elder Board; that he no longer receive a stipend from the church; that his name as pastor be removed from the church sign (the church had gone to a flattened structure and no longer had a head pastor); and that he be required to enter into some intentional therapy to deal with issues of power, sexuality, and the sexual objectification of women.

The Elder Board responded to my requests by saying that they could not hold Andy accountable. He could be accountable only to God. If I wanted him held accountable, I could press legal charges.

I consulted with an attorney experienced in dealing with clergy sexual abuse cases. I found that because there had been no intercourse, I would not be protected by rape laws, and that my whole life could be exposed during a court proceeding. My intent was to sue for therapy costs I had incurred and would probably continue to incur. Given the court's minimal understanding of the issue, I had maybe a fifty-fifty chance of receiving any judgment in my favor.

Denominationally, there was even less recourse. Though he had been licensed as a minister, Andy had never gone through the ordination process of either denomination with which our congregation was affiliated. The formal procedures for recourse through the code of ethics and the sexual harassment/abuse policy were written for ordained clergy. The church had been paying for a rider on its insurance policy covering sexual misconduct, because of the many interns it signed on to work with youth, but I could not access it.

The pain and isolation I felt were nearly unbearable. Church leaders claimed that the problem was my white flight and not sexual abuse. I cried with the psalmist that though my spirit was faint, I believed God knew my path (142:3). However, I wished God would be more forthcoming. I prayed and prayed for God to show me where I needed to ask forgiveness for my part in this mess and what God might ask me to do to repair the brokenness. But God was silent.

During the first few days after I left the church, there were many phone calls back and forth. I remember lying on the couch in the living room, thinking I would never stop crying and fearing I would never sleep again. The hurt inside my heart was so great that I was physically exhausted, every muscle aching as if I'd been beaten. A couple of the elders came over to see me. I physically sat in a chair in the dining room, but mentally I was upstairs in my office, huddled in the corner behind my rocking chair with a blanket over me.

I lost self-respect, self-esteem, dignity, confidence. I lost a community. I lost opportunities for growth and learning. I lost a church home that, for good or ill, I had helped to shape, a home that had encouraged me, challenged me, and caused me to question and work harder than I had ever thought was possible.

Andy's family had been like my own. Since I left the church, he and Ellen have divorced, as have Cynthia and her husband. Andy and Ellen's three children have experienced various kinds of trauma.

IN THE LAST FOUR YEARS my life has changed dramatically. In spite of pain, loss, confusion, and desperation, I can say that God is good—all the time. Many doors have opened to me, giving me an abundance of opportunities for growth and service. I currently serve as an associate minister in an urban African American congregation. There is respect and caring in our relationships, with plenty of good old-fashioned fellowship and laughter. Together we struggle and rejoice as we explore what God is calling us to do and to be.

My present church is a safer place—not perfect, but more protective. It is pastored by a man who treats his spouse and daughter with respect and genuine caring, a man who heeds his auntie's warning, "Don't let your robes drag in the mud," a man who knows my story and has never violated my person. I watched him a long time before I joined the church—how he treated women and girls in the congregation and how he treated men. I gained a pastor and colleague who respects me.

God has also provided me with a new ministry position in a seminary, where I work with students and pastors in experiential education. My experience as a survivor of clergy sexual abuse has contributed to my effectiveness. My intuition has been sharpened, and I have learned to listen to it in my work with students and supervisors. I am also aware of my own personal and professional limitations: that I am not a therapist, a pastoral counselor, a psychologist, or a psychiatrist. I firmly believe in the wisdom of referral. I listen to the alarm bells when they begin ringing, signaling that I am entering dangerous waters and am in over my head.

My call to ministry has been affirmed and confirmed more in the last three or four years than it had been in all of the sixteen prior years. But the greatest blessing has been the people I have the opportunity to work and share with, learn from, walk with, count on, support, laugh with, cry with, challenge, and be challenged by.

Another blessing has been a geographic move. My husband and I moved from the neighborhood that had been my home for sixteen years. Our new home is close to my work and church, close to parks and a big lake, close to new friends. It is symbolic of the changes I have made, as well as tangible evidence of the new life I have been offered.

The consequences of Andy's abuse have been many and far-reaching. All of my primary relationships were tied to him and the church-planting project. I now have a hard time trusting my judgment about people. Have I told you too much? Have I told you anything that you can use to hurt me? Have I held you at arm's length so long that you have given up wanting any kind of friendship with me? I have entered too quickly into some friendships out of loneliness, only to realize later that I had nothing in common with the person. I have also entered friendships only to find out later that I was repeating the same old habits: looking for a big brother, or a mentor, or someone to idealize. I don't trust myself to make good decisions. If one of my deepest relationships has been a sham, does it mean my whole life is a sham? Does it mean that the life I offer to another is worthless? Does it mean so little? Am I capable of having healthy relationships? These questions all seem to lure me into isolation, and I have had to struggle and fight for the will to be part of community.

My experiences with Andy and the church have had repercussions in my marriage. My husband did not resign his position on the Elder Board or leave the church until several months after I left. He said he loved me and would stand with me. However, his support has always been given after careful consideration. In many ways, I feel as if he threw me to the wolves, too. Everyone at the church felt sorry for him because he got "caught in the middle," making me even more the enemy. He told me he didn't want to abandon the children of the church or the youth group. Even after he left, he tithed to the church for a while.

My husband did the best he could with who he was at the time. One of my friends frequently tells me, "Just forgive him," but I don't think it is a matter of forgiveness. Something died. The wounds changed me. My friend wants me to go back to the way things were. I cannot. Is that then "unforgiveness"?

I am left with many questions about myself and my relationships. There are times when having no answers is hard. Yet I stand on the belief that no matter how confused, no matter how painful, no matter how self-serving or self-sacrificing I might be, God is faithful. Somehow in the midst of having no answers, in the midst of feeling guilty, in the midst of shame, in the midst of disappointment, in the midst of anger, in the midst of wanting to forget, in the midst of wanting to flee, God is present with me. Sometimes it is a small comfort, and I do mean small—little, minute. But enough to keep me alive.

Just as my relationships will never be the same, my spiritual life has also been altered. Holy Communion is a difficult ritual for me. For the longest time after I left the church, I couldn't take communion. The Bible says that if you have a problem with a brother or sister, go make the relationship right and then come to the table (Matt. 5:21–26). How could I go to the table? There was no reconciliation; I couldn't make the relationship right. Will I ever again be able to enjoy this community meal? How can I forgive someone who never asked for forgiveness? The closest he came was to say he was sorry he had misread the situation, that maybe there were times when I had come for pastoral care that he treated me like a peer. But he never asked for forgiveness. He said that maybe it had been like emotional rape, but never once was he repentant, sorry for how he had hurt me. He just went on, business as usual, looking for someone else to attend to his needs.

What other consequences have there been? I experience a paradox of memories and blanks. On the one hand, sometimes I will be watching a movie or listening to another woman's story or reading a book, and all these memories will come flooding back over me—so overwhelming that I feel close to being suffocated. On the other hand, there is much I cannot remember. I sit down and look at pictures, look through old worship bulletins, read old sermons, and I still can't remember. I try to reconstruct past incidents of community life, and I can't remember. I have lost part of my life.

Yet I am one of the lucky ones. I did not have intercourse with Andy. And I was not confused over which was Andy and which was God. Some women are hurt so badly by the representative role of the abuser that they can no longer bear God's church, God's people, or even God's self. The collusion of the church and the abuser does so much damage and the abuser is so representative of that higher power that in order to live, a woman must sever all ties with God and faith as she knows it. I was never confused about who Andy was. He was never God for me. But he was someone whose approval and acceptance I wanted and needed.

As I continue to reflect on and process what has happened in my life, I realize I have made changes—some good and some maybe not so good. I have had time to analyze not only what happened in my situation but also how the institutional church colludes and conspires with perpetrators of abuse, and how our culture in general trains and rewards people who take advantage of others. My experience of abuse makes me look at the church and community life in different ways.

I now see that I was seduced not only by the pastor but also by the church community, which became cultlike. The church-planting project started off with much idealism and a strong desire to make a difference. We wanted to break down all the walls that divide people. Consequently, over the years our small church began to operate like it was the one true church, the only church that was taking seriously the brokenness and needs of the world, the one church that was actively involved in making a change. We withdrew from denominational activities and, as a result, became more and more isolated, much as a cult separates itself. The fellowship so clearly identified itself as a community that it became impossible for individuals to have their own dreams of ministry. Such dreams were described as leading one toward being a "Lone Ranger Christian." Outside ideas were suspect.

My experience has also led me to reflect on the manner in which the church handles several issues, among them suffering, "warm fuzzies" in worship, sexuality, power, and authority. Our society will do whatever is necessary to avoid suffering. While the church teaches us to take up the cross, it also tells us to forgive and forget. If we forgive and forget, nobody has to see our suffering and nobody has to walk with us through it. Take two aspirin and call me in the morning. We want quick relief and have very little patience with folks who cannot get on with their life. We treat death this way also. When someone in your family dies, you may get a week off work. When you get back, people will be kind for about another week, but then it's time your grieving is over. It's been four years since I left the church. I should be over it by now. I am way over my two-week grief limit.

Many congregations have a "warm fuzzies" approach to the worship service. When we all get up and pass the peace, I don't want to hug everyone. Sometimes I will offer my hand, only to have a man bigger and stronger pull me into an embrace. Where is my choice? Where is my bodily integrity? Trying to claim my own space can create an awkward situation.

My experience with Andy has also led me to reflect on sexuality and the church. Sexuality is present in every relationship, though the church sometimes acts as if it didn't exist at all. We are afraid of its power and so ignore it, as if somehow we are only spiritual beings who transcend our humanness. We have to get to a place where we acknowledge and celebrate our whole selves, without compartmentalizing. I think we are afraid to recognize sexuality in our relationships because we think sexuality has to do with only our genitals. But ignoring the power of sexuality can then lead our clergy—any of us—into situations where we say, "Well, I just couldn't help it. I couldn't control myself." The gift of sexuality is a gift only when it honors self and other.

As one who educates and has responsibilities for training ministers, I don't joke about sex with students or colleagues. I don't use sexual innuendo, nor do I tolerate it. I don't even allow students to call me or others "Honey" or "Sweetie." I value clarity and forthrightness. If someone is talking about sex, then it needs to be up front. No cutesy, flirtatious nonsense. I am very clear about boundary issues. I don't mince words with students about their responsibilities as ministers.

The church needs to wrestle with issues of authority and power. What does it mean to have authority as a pastor? What do we ministers do when others endow us with more power than we want? We need to take seriously how we influence others, for good or for ill. It is trendy for pastors to take authority lightly, to claim that we are no different from anyone else or that we don't want to perpetuate a hierarchical system. However, in this imperfect world, we need to be mindful of others' understanding of pastoring and of the ways in which power and authority enter the pastoral relationship.

I know I will never "get over" my experience. I was a vulnerable young person who trusted a pastor/teacher/mentor/supervisor to have my best interests at heart. After he was through with me or got tired of waiting for a sexual consummation, I watched him sexualize another relationship. To my regret, I did nothing about it; I was so glad he was someone else's problem that I didn't warn her. I trusted a church that revictimized me—made me the villain, didn't believe me, didn't trust my perception. When everyone you love tells you you're wrong, it is incredibly difficult to believe in yourself.

My losses are innumerable. I lost a church, a family, a community. I lost all that I was familiar with and thought I loved. I lost a bundle of money on counseling. But with many of the losses came breakthroughs. I lost naïveté and innocence but gained more honest relationships. I lost answers and rules for ordering my life, all the right and wrong ways to think and live and act; but I am learning to be guided by relationships with God and others rather than by rules. I lost my identity, my childhood, my life as I knew it; but I am finding myself, my identity, my gifts and graces in new ways. I lost my moorings, my groundings; but I have discovered the adventure of setting out into the deep. In a way I lost God; but maybe the God I lost was not a true God, merely one created by someone else. I seek the God who desires a relationship with me.

Sometimes I want to scream, "Yes, I am a victim of clergy sexual abuse!" Yes, it did happen to me. I hate the secret. I hate the burden. Why can't I talk about this the way one would talk about any other injustice? But I can't, probably because I fear there will always be someone who thinks I asked for it or wanted it.

But in many ways I am no longer a victim. I don't even want to use the word "survivor," because I don't want just to survive. I want to live and thrive. And I am thriving—despite what happened, despite the pain, despite the shame I feel, despite the secret.

Andy took the gift of my life and treated it like refuse, rubbish, trash. But somewhere, in a tiny room of my soul, I kept just a little of me for myself. And that tiny seed is going to live and grow and thrive and produce fruit and nourish others. I will not let the victimized part of my life own me, define me, or kill me. I will not let the Andys of this world win. My God is more powerful and more loving than the likes of these.

No, I will never get over it. There are daily reminders of the brokenness and scars. I have no assurances about the future, about my marriage, about other friendships and relationships. I know that down the road there may be more pain and hurt that is directly or indirectly related to this history of mine. But I am convinced that God will be present even in silence and that I will be whole.

CHAPTER SIX

Even the Stones Will Cry Out

LINDSEY

The church, founded upon the Rock and called to do justice, did its job and did it well. My hope is that by telling my story I will help others within the church to respond to the cries of those abused by clergy.

I can see it now. I wish I had been able to see then that Grant Bailey was grooming me for his own desires. He always made it sound as if he was trying to help my marriage. He was patient. It took nearly two years for the relationship to become fully sexual. By then he had me hooked. I would have given up anything for him at that point. Why? At least four factors in my life made me vulnerable to him.

I was born right after World War II to parents who were grieving. Mama had lost her first husband in the war. Daddy had lost a wife and daughter to divorce and another daughter to death. My birth as an identical twin gave my family reason for double joy, but only three months after our births, my twin sister died of pneumonia. I represented hope. As a result, by the time a sister and brother were born, I had already developed the need to relieve others' suffering. That deep, primitive need inside me must have unconsciously responded to Grant, whom I now recognize as being a sick man.

Second, I grew up in a culture that did not value women as much as men. Though no female in my nuclear or extended family had an education beyond high school, I had a strong desire to go to college. My parents said they could afford to send only one child, and it would have to be their only son, my younger brother. I compromised by accepting my parents' plan for me to go to nursing school, but I didn't relish the idea of becoming a nurse. Though I did well academically and socially, I quit in my senior year to follow my new husband's military calling. This was my cultural and biblical role as I understood it. Men's work was more valuable.

My father's dying wish was for me to finish my nurse's training. I didn't finish, but I long felt the powerfully ingrained pull to put my own desires aside to fulfill those of a strong male authority. This attitude prepared me for later accepting the authority of another strong male figure.

The question of vocational call remained with me for a long time. Though I loved being a mom and homemaker, there was always something inside me wanting to be more and do more. If I had been male, I would have chosen ministry. Since my theology said God didn't call women, I could only be a helpmate to God's work. Grant used to say how much I helped him; I was the only one he could talk with. He took my desire to serve God and others and used it for himself.

A third factor making me vulnerable was the judgmental theology of my childhood, which no longer made sense when I got older. As a child I attended church on Sunday mornings and evenings, on Wednesday nights, and whenever there was a program for my age group. If there was a week's revival, I was present every night. I went to church because I wanted to, not because I was made to go. For me, God was personal. However, during adolescence I could no longer accept the judgmental theology men preached to me week after week. I wanted to worship where grace and love were the basis of faith, not where you had to fear eternal hell if you broke one of the rules.

When I married Robert, my high school sweetheart, and joined his church in a different denomination, I found a group that ap-

proached the world with a spirit of love and openness. Three years
after our marriage and soon after we moved to a new town, we
began to worship at the church where Grant was pastor. I eagerly
listened to his messages of love. "You know," I heard a friend tell
him once, "I have listened to you preach for years now and you
only give one sermon. It's about love." This was true. According to
Grant, God's love was limitless, without restriction. There were no
boundaries, no exclusions. I believed him.

The fourth contributor to my vulnerability was my unsatisfy-
ing relationship with my husband. Like many men of his genera-
tion, Robert went to work, provided for the family, and puttered
in the garage. What else was there to marriage? I had more needs
than that. I wanted to share stories of our day, take an occasional
walk, hold hands in public, sometimes give a spontaneous kiss.
But I received little physical and emotional attention, and what I
offered got a cool reception. Between Robert's job and National
Guard duty, he was gone most of the time. Our two children
were preschoolers. I was lonely in the new town and starved for
attention. My vulnerabilities made me an easy target for Grant's
exploitation.

When Robert and I had been members of the church for about
a year, Grant approached us about joining a group he was orga-
nizing. The group comprised six young married couples and Grant,
who made it clear that he was not the leader of the group but one
of us. The group's purpose was vague. We never prayed or worshiped together. At our weekly meetings we talked about our lives,
our good and bad times.

Grant encouraged physical closeness. We hugged a lot, rubbed
each other's shoulders, and sat holding hands, not always with
our partner. Desiring physical intimacy as I did, I was very aware
of Grant's nearness when he started sitting next to me most of
the time. Sometimes he sat with his arm around my shoulder and
his legs turned toward me, a behavior I would have liked from my
husband. Grant's actions confused me, but no one said anything,

not even Robert. Maybe I was being prudish, I thought. I should learn to relax and enjoy the attention. Besides, I had been raised never to question men in authority, especially preachers and doctors.

About a year into these sessions, Grant announced that he would be leaving the group to start another one. His leaving saddened me, as I had come to enjoy the apparently innocent physical attention I got from him. After his last meeting with the group, out in the parking lot, Grant came to my side of the car just before I got in. Robert was already waiting inside the car. Grant gave me a hug, one so robust that he lifted me off the ground. He held me close and whispered in my ear, "I'm going to be seeing more of you." His hug and words were both thrilling and confusing. I knew not to tell Robert what had happened. Later I told myself I was probably making too much of a simple statement.

Soon after that night, Grant told me he was going to recommend to the nominating committee that I become a member of the congregation's ruling body. But women couldn't be leaders in the church, I told myself. The Bible said so, and my mother said so. After many weeks of considering the possibility of God sometimes calling women to leadership positions, I decided to serve if elected. I was elected. I am certain that Grant manipulated the process just as he manipulated many other decisions made in that church.

Being ordained into the leadership of the church awakened a feeling that had been lying dormant inside me since high school. Although God *was* perhaps involved in extending the call, I now understand this period as part of Grant's strategy. He saw my hunger to serve God. He had the power and position to offer me opportunities to participate in the church in ways I had never dreamed possible. However, I don't remember Grant's talking to me about my calling or about how God was working in my life. Our conversations were always about my importance in Grant's life.

Though I preferred community outreach, Grant thought I would learn more on the worship committee. Several times a week, I dropped off my daughter at the church nursery school and stopped by Grant's office to discuss worship. We would briefly handle business, then he would turn to personal questions. I don't remember exactly what the questions were, only that they gently probed for the details of my life. Our conversations went something like this:

"Well, how are you feeling today?" Grant would ask.

I stumbled over words, because it was a question I wasn't used to being asked. No one else seemed to care.

Then, "How's Robert?"

"Working hard," I probably said. "He'll be gone again this weekend. Seems like we don't see each other much."

"How are you and Robert doing? Are you happy?"

Never having had much personal contact with a pastor, I thought this was probably what a pastoral relationship was like. I thought Grant genuinely cared about Robert and me. So as time progressed and Grant asked questions about my marriage, I thought I was receiving comfort and guidance.

Several times he told me how close he had come to getting a Ph.D. in psychology. All he needed to do, he said, was rewrite his dissertation, but he had become involved with his family and ministry and had decided to forgo the degree. Supposedly this explained why he understood psychological matters and was such a good counselor.

One day Grant had two tickets to preview a movie. The theater had given matinee tickets to area ministers to get their feedback. Since Grant's wife had to work, did I want to go along? I was flattered. Later I told Robert about going to the movie; I didn't tell him what happened afterward.

I parked at the church and rode with Grant. When we returned to the church, he asked if I could come in for a few minutes to discuss the film. This time he didn't want to go to his office but to a more isolated room. Though I wondered why, I wasn't in-clined to question male authority. Facing each other on fold-up chairs, we talked about the film. Suddenly he extended his hand and said, "Come here." He pulled me onto his lap and began kissing me passionately. Though the sexual part of me wanted to respond, I pushed him back. He held on to me, gently asking what I felt.

"I don't know how anything that feels so good could be so bad."

"It's not bad."

"But I'm married and so are you."

"Think about it and we'll talk later."

And talk we did, for more than a year. Meanwhile, I felt affirmed by Grant's confidence in my abilities and by his expressions of how important I was to him. As I look back, however, I see that my sense of self-worth was diminishing. I came to count on his opinions about life, religion, and the pursuit of my happiness. I quit thinking for myself. Through a slow process of indoctrina-tion and brainwashing, a perpetrator manipulates a victim to change attitudes and beliefs. The subtlety of Grant's manipula-tions still amazes me. As we talked I was reminded that Robert didn't appreciate me, that Robert didn't know what I needed. But Grant knew and he offered it.

At first our conversations ended with hugs, then with brief kisses that eventually turned into light petting that turned into heavy petting. I resisted going any further; he continued trying to persuade me. Then he used an argument that caused me to pause and wonder and pray: he said sex with him would be the best thing for my marriage. He knew my marriage was in serious trouble. When I told him sex between us would be wrong, he responded that love was never wrong. I said it had to be more than not wrong; it had to be right. Keep thinking about it, he urged me.

I prayed my most desperate prayer to God: "Help me. Show me. I know my marriage is right in your eyes. If this is what I have to do to help it, then not my will but thine be done." But God was silent. Only Grant's voice came through. Finally I succumbed to Grant's will, and soon I thought it was my own will as well.

During the next two years we had occasional sexual intercourse. I suspected I was not the only woman. "Just friendly," he said of the hugs and kisses I saw him give two other women. At the same time he suggested I should be more open toward relationships with other men. I should also encourage Robert to develop closer friendships with other women. It would be good for him and for our marriage. So I promoted Robert's friendship with my best friend, Sue, while at the same time Grant sanctioned my friendship with Sue's husband. That these relationships got out of control is partly the responsibility of the persons involved; however, I mainly hold Grant responsible for coaching from the sidelines and applauding the overinvolvement.

A denominational leader, Grant began opening doors of opportunity for me. When the national denomination began a project, it appointed leaders in each of the states to carry out the project. Grant appointed me to the position in our state, pleasing me with his confidence. At his suggestion, I set up an office in one of the buildings on the church property. I didn't see that the location would make me more available to him.

I was also nominated and elected to be on a church committee at the state level. Both of these duties required me to travel to meetings that Grant also sometimes attended. By now, I wanted to spend more time with him, but he wasn't available to me at these out-of-town meetings.

Did I think I was in love? Definitely, absolutely. It was the greatest love I had ever known, love so great that it scared me for a while, because I would have given up my kids and my husband for him. It still scares me to think how dangerous some so-called love can be.

Over time I became increasingly disillusioned with our relationship. If our love was all right, why was it a secret? "Because," he would answer, "if people knew, they wouldn't understand. It could destroy my career and their faith." I didn't want to be responsible for destroying the faith of anyone. Years later I considered the other part of his statement: "It could destroy my career." What about my life? Didn't he see that this relationship had *not* helped my marriage as he had said it would?

I hated the secret. It gnawed at my marriage and at my self-esteem. I wanted to end the sexual relationship with Grant, but I didn't want his support and encouragement for my growth to stop. Besides, to break out of the secret, I needed to tell someone. Grant had often assured me that he was widely respected and that if I told, he would have to deny our relationship to protect many other people. I knew I couldn't stand up against his social and political power. Compared to him, who was I? He did say that he would understand if I someday needed to talk with a therapist. In the meantime, however, I was to talk with him and no one else. Though I had no words then for his admonition to keep quiet, I now recognize his efforts to isolate me.

I was relieved when Robert told me we were moving again. I was ready to clear my plate of Grant and all the committee work I was deeply involved in. With the move, I thought I would be free from several impediments to my marriage. I would be free from the sexual relationship with Grant and from the relationship that had developed between my husband and my best friend. I would be free from my attraction to her husband, an attraction Grant had encouraged by saying that I was capable of loving more than one man and that I should. I wanted to start over with only my husband and my family, which now included a third daughter, whom we had adopted.

Starting over didn't happen the way I hoped. Grant soon manipulated his way into a job as chaplain of a local college in my new town. He was still my pastor and friend, he told me, and he would still be my lover if I wanted. The choice was mine. And if I ever needed him, I could just call. I did call.

My mother telephoned early one morning to say that my uncle, who had been a surrogate father to me, had died. Robert was returning from a business trip. His parents, who lived out of town, were staying in our house. Sue was coming to visit because she said she had to see Robert. Life seemed terribly out of balance. My desire to rebuild my marriage with a fresh start was crumbling before we had even started. I called Grant, asking him if we could talk. Sex was the last thing on my mind. I needed him now as pastor and friend.

When Grant arrived that evening, the children were in bed and Robert's parents were in their bedroom. Tearfully, I told Grant about my uncle and about my fear that something was going on between Robert and Sue. He flippantly said I could handle it all. If Robert and Sue loved each other, I should remember that love was good. By the way, he said, he had something to tell me.

A story began to unfold about another woman he had met, a younger and very beautiful woman. He had never felt like that toward any woman before. By this time I must have been practically dissociated. By that I mean I could barely hear what he was saying. The room around me seemed unreal. Life was spinning out of control. I had lost my surrogate father, I was losing my husband, and I was losing my best friend. Now I didn't even have a friend in Grant anymore. He had said he would always be there for me, but now he couldn't even hear me. All he wanted to do was tell me about this other woman, a woman he claimed that I, too, would come to love. Suddenly he pushed me over on the couch and tried to make love. My kids and my in-laws were all in the house. Besides, I didn't want sex with him. When I said so, he said goodbye. He was angry.

Going through the motions of saying goodbye, I felt empty and lost, emotionally and spiritually destroyed. My world was closing in around and within me. From the window I watched him walk across the street to his car. I climbed the stairs and went into the bedroom. Robert would be home the following day, and Sue would be there to see him. How was I going to save myself, to save us? Grant had trained me for several years to count on him, and now I couldn't. I lay on my bed weeping. There were no thoughts, no prayers, just raw, primitive weeping. And aloneness.

When Sue arrived the next day, I was jealous. I tried to follow Grant's advice to give her and Robert time and space. I was still listening to Grant instead of to myself. Robert and Sue sat up late that night while I stayed down the hall, alone in the bedroom and wide awake. Midnight came, then one o'clock, two o'clock. At around three, I could stand it no longer. I wanted to know what was going on down the hall. I walked into the room where they sat apart from each other, but the room was dark and the music romantic. Without speaking, I turned and walked back to the bedroom and into the bathroom. My legs no longer supported me. I collapsed on the floor, sobbing into a towel because I didn't want anyone to hear me. If I really loved Robert and Sue, I was supposed to bear this hurt. Grant had told me repeatedly, "Love is never wrong." I don't know how long I lay there before Robert came in and tried to lift me. I had no strength. I remember little of what happened in the next hours and days, only that I was surprised at the enormous level of fatigue I felt. Nearly a decade later, I learned that Robert and Sue had in fact been having an affair.

Grant got a divorce and moved the new woman, along with her three children, into his house. Eventually I met the woman, Lynn. Grant was right about one thing: I did come to love her as a friend. He had not anticipated that I would also come to love her as a sister who had experienced abuse by the same trusted man.

The next seven years were filled with family, school, and church committee work. I returned to college. I began by studying the subjects that interested me: religion and psychology. I went on to complete a graduate degree in clinical social work. About ten years later, I was the clinical director in a pastoral counseling center, a position I still hold.

Robert and I sought marriage counseling and stayed with it for more than a year. Neither Grant's nor Sue's name ever came up. Even though I wanted my marriage to my high school sweetheart and the father of my children to work, we eventually divorced. I have often wondered if the divorce could have been avoided had we gotten the help we needed early in our marriage. Both of us are now remarried, and we socialize in activities involving our children, grandchildren, and mutual friends.

A turning point in my life occurred the day I told my therapist about the affair I had had with my pastor. "It wasn't an affair," she told me. She explained my relationship with Grant as being something like a father's abuse of a child. I started to read everything I could get my hands on about the topic, which wasn't much. There was a lot about child abuse but not much about abuse by clergy.

As a result of my studies, I began to understand my relationship with Grant much differently. Having previously thought of it as consensual, I now saw the imbalance of power. Grant had had power not only because of his role as pastor but also because he was male and big. At the time he was also better educated, with more social connections and prestige. Yet he had denied the disparity, because he had "leveled the playing field." If a man and a woman are peers, there is no need to pretend to be leveling the field.

As I learned more, I knew that filing a complaint against Grant was a possibility but not a realistic one. There were no policies or procedures in our denomination for making allegations of clergy sexual abuse.

One day I was discussing the need for guidelines with two members of the clergy, one the incoming leader of our judicatory. We agreed that our judicatory could write its own policy and procedures and that we didn't need to wait for the national body to do the job. I volunteered to serve on a committee to develop a policy and was later asked to be the chair. In the course of our work, I hinted at my abuse to the executive who worked with us. On the day our document was passed by the voting body, as the executive and I walked out into the fresh air, he said, "I know a little about what this means to you. How do you feel?"

"Redeemed," I responded. "Now no other woman has to suffer in silence for lack of procedures." Tears of relief rolled down my cheeks.

I went on with my life, which included not only my children but also a new career and a new husband. When I told him about the abuse, he couldn't understand it as abuse. He thought he couldn't trust me. I am sorry to say his attitude about my experience never changed. We had been married four years when he suddenly died of acute congestive heart failure.

Prior to his death, I learned that the denomination at the highest level had removed all statutes of limitation on reporting clergy sexual abuse. At the time I first heard, I didn't want to file charges. The "Grant thing," as I had come to call the experience, had ruined one marriage. I didn't want it interfering with another any more than it already had. But after my husband died and I had worked through much of my grief, I began to reconsider.

In the meantime I had become a close friend of Lynn, the woman Grant had told me about. Together we tried to sort through the way Grant had entangled right and wrong, truth and lies, good and evil. We talked about reporting him, because we knew he had left the college to work in another state at a residential treatment facility for emotionally disturbed adolescent girls.

Memories of an anecdote he'd told our couples' group on more than one occasion kept coming back to me. In his efforts to help his adolescent daughter feel comfortable with her body, he would enter the bathroom when she was in the tub. She always protested. One day he proudly announced to the group that she finally accepted her body. He knew this was so because when he'd entered the bathroom, she'd said nothing. More likely, he never heard her silent scream, "I give up. I have no privacy with you around." Some would say it's a stretch to call this abusive behavior. At a minimum, I would call it sexually inappropriate. As I remembered Grant's story, I kept telling myself he had no access to the girls at the facility; his job was to raise funds.

About a year after my second husband's death, I started to see John, a man in my Rotary Club chapter. Over dinner one evening, we discussed a movie we'd seen the night before. "I've never met anyone in my life so manipulative," he said of the movie's main character. "Have you?"

My heart rate picked up. I felt hot. My mouth went dry. How much did I dare say? The "Grant thing" had already caused trouble in two marriages.

But I heard myself saying, "Yes."

"You have?"

"Oh yes, I have no trouble at all believing someone can be that manipulative. I've experienced it." Oh, shit, I thought. Why did I say that?

"What happened?"

I was hesitant. I felt a choking sensation in my throat and was light-headed. "I'm not sure I want to talk about it." I said.

He was calm. I reminded myself that he wasn't my husband, and if he ever were to be, I should find out ahead of time how he would react to this information about my life. Besides, as a doctor, he knew about power relationships between himself and his patients. Only recently, he had gone to another seminar on the subject. Deciding to test the waters, I told him a little. Soon I had said much more than I had intended. He was so compassionate and such a good listener that I had just kept talking.

"Why don't you report him?" he asked rather matter-of-factly.

I was speechless. Tears of relief washed over me. When we walked back to the car, I had not yet responded to the question. I was to drive the car, but when we got in, I just sat there, unable to start the engine. Finally I asked, "If I couldn't bring myself to report him, what would you think of me?"

He said he wouldn't think less of me, but this man needed to be stopped and he needed to be held accountable.

"You mean you could be supportive of me if I reported him?"

"Of course."

"I'll think about it, then." Something within me was released.

Seated at my computer several days later, I typed a letter to the appropriate person. I knew the procedures, having helped write them. "I'll join you," Lynn said when I told her what I had done. "This is something we need to do."

When I told my former husband Robert that I was filing a church complaint against Grant, his response surprised me. He held Grant responsible for destroying our marriage and realized that he, too, had been Grant's victim. His words helped bring further healing in that he could see beyond blaming me or himself.

I WAS IN THE BEDROOM when the phone rang. "I received your letter," the church leader said. "All that work you did, and I didn't know. First, on behalf of the church, in my position as one of its leaders, I want to apologize for the harm that has occurred in your life."

Deeply moved, I sat down on the edge of the bed. I had not anticipated the healing power such words could offer. I was willing to quit the process then and there; his words were enough. He did not question my letter. My truth. He did not ask, "Are you sure this is accurate?" or "Are you sure you want to go through with it?" The leader's simple but profound acceptance of me, my story, and my pain touched me deeply. He went on to explain carefully what the next steps would be. He gave me his home phone number so that if I had any questions, I could call him confidentially without going through his office, where I knew everyone.

First Grant had to be found, because he had moved to a new jurisdiction far away. Then my letter would be forwarded to the executive there. I waited two weeks, then three. Finally I received a phone call from a judicatory leader, who explained the delay. Grant had retired and moved again, this time to her jurisdiction, three thousand miles from where I lived and from where the abuse had taken place. She offered compassion and concern, told me she would appoint a committee to investigate, and said my next call would come from the chair of the committee.

I waited. Several times I considered stopping the procedure. Yet Grant had not yet been held accountable, and in my counseling practice I had encouraged and empowered women. I knew I had to be able to do for myself what I would want another to do for herself. Furthermore, my relationship with John had continued, and he supported my persevering.

When the investigating committee chair, Kenneth, called to introduce himself and to lay out the plan, I had one important question for him: "Does this committee have any knowledge and training about clergy sexual abuse?" He wouldn't answer me directly, so I feared it did not. I emphasized the importance of this knowledge in seeking justice. I do not believe that education tips the scales in favor of the victim; on the contrary, it balances the scales. I recommended some books.

We agreed upon a date for the committee's conference-call deposition. Kenneth sent a photograph ahead of time so that I could put faces to the people I'd be talking with.

On the day of the call, I was anxious and suspicious, not knowing whether I could trust the committee. For three and a half hours I answered questions posed by an attorney. The conversation was formal and legal. (During the ensuing months of the investigation, this attention to a tight legal process gave me security and comfort.) I even had to be sworn in before the questioning began. The committee wanted details. It wanted chronology. I was emotionally exhausted afterward.

After questioning many other people, the committee decided to file charges against Grant on behalf of the church. As many victims do, I sometimes questioned my own story. Was it my imagination? Did I remember events correctly? Maybe what happened hadn't been so bad after all. Maybe it was my fault. Church leaders, however, had decided that my charges presented a serious matter. What more could I ask? By believing me and by seeking justice, the church affirmed me and moved me further toward growth and healing.

The church's investigation continued for nearly a year. Committee members talked to people whose names Lynn and I had given them and to others they learned about on their own. Even Robert had an opportunity to tell his story. Kenneth kept me informed about the committee's work and expressed concern for me. Sometimes I felt uneasy about how nice he was. I finally explained to him that as a result of the abuse, I did not trust compliments, encouragement, or niceness from men. Grant had used the same style to seduce me. Kenneth proved to be patient with my skittishness.

When talks of a negotiated settlement arose, I was ambivalent. I wasn't sure justice could really be served without a trial. Kenneth kept assuring me that the committee would not agree to a settlement that was not comfortable for both Lynn and me. His assurance was gracious and respectful and empowering.

Nevertheless, Lynn and I did not agree to the settlement, and a court date was set. Robert agreed to come along as my witness. I experienced his willingness as an eloquent expression of forgiving me. I remained in continual prayer and hope that this process was in some way healing for him too.

In its thoroughness, the committee lined up as witnesses some of the country's leading experts in clergy sexual abuse. It also hired a first-rate prosecuting attorney with knowledge and experience in the field and in church court processes. The committee had learned from firsthand experience what a manipulator Grant could be. It was prepared for all arguments that he and his attorney might pose.

Church courts are not civil or criminal courts. Our denomination is governed by a constitution, which mandates policies and procedures in situations of abuse or conflict. The preliminary investigation had led the committee to believe the charges were serious enough for the church to seek justice through a complete investigation, culminating in a trial if necessary. Seven elected members make up the judicial commission, which hears cases. The members have no prior knowledge of a case, and when they hear it, they act as judge and jury. If the defendant loses the case, it can be appealed to the next level of church court. The "sentencing," or terms of discipline, is also decided by the court. This judicial process is taken as seriously as a civil suit and trial.

In this case, the defendant was responsible for his own expenses. The judicatory bore the cost of Lynn's and my case, though our attorney volunteered much of his time and none of the committee members were paid. Our expenses for airfare, hotel accommodations, and telephone calls, plus the cost for lost time at work for Lynn, me, and our witnesses, were paid by the judicatory. This amazed me, since Grant had only recently moved there and was retired. When I expressed my gratitude for the financial responsibility the church was shouldering, Kenneth reminded me that I had paid plenty; it was now the church's turn to bear the cost of doing justice. It helped me to remember that my job was to be a primary witness for the church in its efforts to preserve the integrity of ministry, to uphold truth, to protect other victims, and to hold Grant accountable.

Lynn, our two witnesses, and I arrived in a blinding snowstorm. A committee member met us at the airport and took us to a hotel, where I had a chance to think, pray, and prepare for the next few days. Each of us had been given a folder welcoming us and outlining the upcoming activities. Included in the written remarks was this sentence: "Even though we realize that nobody would choose to be here, we want you to remember our city as a hospitable place and our judicatory as a place where you felt welcome." Such was the hospitality we received.

The day of preparation for the trial began by greeting in person the people we had become familiar with by name only. The chair, Kenneth, led us in an informal worship service the committee had prepared. We, the guests, were each given a stone from the local river. "Luke 19:36–40" was painted on each stone, and "I tell you, if these were silent, the stones would shout out." Kenneth connected the history of the local stones to the abuse of the indigenous ancestors of that area. Referring to Lynn's and my experience, he said that this, too, was the time for even the stones to cry out. I felt deeply loved by God and the church. Nothing in this expression of love was intended to harm. This was active love that sought justice.

The day of the trial arrived. I would soon see Grant, and after all the years, I didn't know what to expect. The women of the committee would not let Lynn or me leave the room without them, in case we ran into him. They fussed over us a bit. "Do you need to go the rest room? Do you want something to eat or drink?" They were making sure we felt as safe and secure as possible.

Even at these last moments, Grant's attorney was trying to reach an out-of-trial settlement. Our team entered the courtroom first. Seated next to Lynn, I reached over to hold her hand. We had not yet seen Grant. I was curious about what he would look like and how I would feel seeing him again. Then he seemed to appear from out of nowhere. He walked directly in front of my chair with his new wife and his attorney. No one spoke.

Grant looked old and worn-out. The year had probably been hard on him. He never believed he would get caught. He had told Lynn many times that no one would ever have the nerve to report him. But here he was before us. I wasn't scared of him, but I was anxious about the process. The attorneys announced to the judicial committee that they had reached a proposed settlement if the court would approve. Events were moving fast.

Slouched back in the chair, Grant had one arm on the table, the other thrown over the back of the chair. His legs were stretched out in front of him, spread somewhat apart. What an arrogant body posture, I thought.

The first time a member of the judicial committee asked Grant a question, he grabbed it as an opportunity to stand and address the court. He explained that he had been sexually abused as a child and that he had spent time working on it in therapy. He would not admit he had harmed anyone, but if he had, he was sorry. He was no longer the same person he had been twenty-five years ago. Our attorney rose to stop this spontaneous speech, and his attorney pulled on Grant's jacket to get him to sit down.

Grant would sign the agreement only if the plea was nolo contendere, which meant he would not admit guilt but would submit himself to punishment as though he had pleaded guilty. We were hesitant to agree to this, but his statement did say, "He accepts as true the facts set forth in these charges and specifications, and he agrees to the terms of censure which have been proposed." There were five single-spaced pages of charges and censure. Moving into an executive session, the judicial commission returned with a decision to accept nolo contendere with a revision. A definition of nolo contendere would be acceptable to all parties, including a statement of Grant's admission of wrongdoing and repentance.

I nearly jumped out of my seat. Repentance! Repentance is about admitting wrongs and attempting to make amends. Grant had never shown any sign of repentance, not to me, not to my family, not to Lynn. We deliberated among ourselves and offered the word "remorse" in place of repentance. It was accepted.

Next the commission called the attorneys to the bench. Ours returned to tell us, "The commission wants to give you a chance to speak. You can say anything you want."

I had come prepared only to answer questions. Quickly, however, I decided that I wanted to speak. Lynn and I went together to sit in two chairs that faced both the commission and Grant. I was glad there was a small table to rest my arms on. Someone set a box of tissue on the table.

I don't remember all I said. At first tears filled my eyes. But as I talked I felt myself becoming stronger. Finally I looked Grant in the eyes and said, "Grant Bailey lied to me about the truth of the gospel of Jesus Christ. He lied to me about the meaning of love. He seduced me into a relationship with him, making me believe it would be good for my marriage. My marriage ended and my former husband is here today. He is prepared to give his side of how this abuse affected our family." Later, back at home and work, I found renewed strength in remembering myself looking into Grant's eyes and saying, "He lied to me."

The proceedings adjourned. We had traveled far to cry out, to bring expert testimony. We weren't emotionally ready simply to walk away from one another. So we didn't. The committee ordered lunch for all who were there as witnesses and representatives of the church. As we sat informally in a circle, our attorney suggested that he could ask some of the questions he had prepared so that witnesses could speak. We listened to each other's perspectives. We needed this debriefing time together.

Today I do remember that city for its love and hospitality.

Grant did not stop trying to manipulate. Even before we left town, he called our attorney and members of the committee that would be responsible for overseeing him. He was busy making contacts. He even tried to get the whole decision thrown out, but he failed.

I USED TO KNOW GOD through the voice of a "man of God" and through his interpretation of scripture. I now know God in many other ways. I know God through my clients' lives and their stories of suffering and healing. Through my inquisitive four-year-old grandson's questions and abundant joy of life. Through my infant grandson's spontaneous total body smile when he sees me. I know God through the constancy of the seasons year after year.

And I know God through the church's willingness to seek justice.

Resources

Contributors to this book have found the following resources helpful to individuals and congregations.

Books

Bradshaw, John. *Healing the Shame That Binds You.* Deerfield Beach, Fla.: Health Communications, 1988.

Brady, Maureen. *Daybreak: Meditations for Women Survivors of Sexual Abuse.* Center City, Minn.: Hazelden, 1991.

Crossing the Boundary: Professional Sexual Abuse. Akron, Pa.: Mennonite Central Committee, 1991.

Ells, Albert. *A New Beginning: Daily Devotions for Women Survivors of Sexual Abuse.* Nashville: Nelson, 1992.

Fortune, Marie M. *Is Nothing Sacred?* Cleveland: The Pilgrim Press, 1999.

————. *Sexual Violence—The Unmentionable Sin: An Ethical and Pastoral Perspective.* Cleveland: The Pilgrim Press, 1983.

Heggen, Carolyn Holderread. *Sexual Abuse in Christian Homes and Churches.* Scottdale, Pa.: Herald Press, 1993.

Hopkins, Nancy, and Mark Laaser, eds. *Restoring the Soul of a Church: Congregations Wounded by Clergy Sexual Misconduct.* Bethesda, Md.: Alban Institute, 1995.

Johnson, David, and Jeff VanVonderen. *The Subtle Power of Spiritual Abuse.* Minneapolis: Bethany House, 1991.

Lebacqz, Karen, and Ronald Barton. *Sex in the Parish.* Louisville: Westminster/John Knox, 1991.

Morrison, Jan. *A Safe Place: Beyond Sexual Abuse.* Wheaton, Ill.: Shaw, 1990.

Peck, M. Scott. *The Road Less Traveled: A New Psychology of Love, Traditional Values, and Spiritual Growth.* New York: Simon & Schuster, 1998.

Quinn, Phil E. *From Victim to Victory: Prescriptions from a Survivor of Child Abuse.* Nashville: Abingdon, 1994.

Rutter, Peter. *Sex in the Forbidden Zone.* New York: Fawcett, 1997.

————. *Sex, Power, and Boundaries: Understanding and Preventing Sexual Harassment.* New York: Bantam, 1996.

Sumrall, Amber Coverdale, and Dena Taylor, eds. *Sexual Harassment: Women Speak Out.* Freedom, Calif.: Crossing, 1992.

Winters, Mary S. *Laws against Sexual and Domestic Violence: A Concise Guide for Clergy and Laity.* Cleveland: The Pilgrim Press, 1988.

VIDEOS

Not in My Church (1991)

Once You Cross the Line (1991)

Both are available from the Center for the Prevention of Sexual and Domestic Violence, 936 North Thirty-fourth Street, Suite 200, Seattle, Washington 98103.